In the Morning

In the Morning

Reflections from First Light

Philip Lee Williams

Mercer University Press
Macon, Georgia

ISBN 978-0-88146-022-3
MUP/H717

Published by
Mercer University Press
1400 Coleman Avenue
Macon, Georgia 31207

First Edition.

The essay "History Mornings" appeared in a slightly different
form in *LOST Magazine*.

The paper used in this publication meets the minimum
requirements of American National Standard for Information
Sciences—Permanence of Paper for Printed Library Materials,
ANSI Z39.48-1992.

Library of Congress Cataloging-in-Publication Data

Williams, Philip Lee.
In the morning : reflections from first light/
Philip Lee Williams. --
1st ed. p. cm.
A collection of essays.
ISBN-13: 978-0-88146-022-3
(hardcover : alk. paper)
ISBN-10: 0-88146-022-2
(hardcover : alk. paper)
I. Title.
PS3573.I45535I6 2006
814'.54—dc22
2006013980

This book is for Megan Leigh Williams

Contents

First Things

Morning rose gray and warm today on Wildcat Ridge. An owl not 40 feet from the front door cried over and over just before dawn, a wild feral shriek, warning, or omen. Now, just after 8:00 A.M. in early June, in the dripping woods of north central Georgia, the promise of storms has turned the day still and silent. Chattering squirrels have gone solemn. The light of day seeps to the forest floor, uncertain but insistent.

Morning. Each day the world yawns with light as the planet comes out of its spin away from the sun. It heralds the wedding day of two lovers, the funeral of a beloved father or mother, the hope of good news, the punishment of a hangover, or the start of a journey.

And yet morning has had few books all its own. Poets and children's authors love to use "morning" in their titles. Poet Ted Kooser wrote a book called *Winter Morning Walks*. Indian author Jerome Fourstar wrote *How the Morning and Evening Stars Came to Be: An Assoniboine Story*. Eighteenth-century writer Thomas Letchworth penned *A Morning and Evening's Meditation, Or A Descant on the Times*, printed by none other than Benjamin Franklin. Contemporary poet and NPR commentator Andrei Codrescu authored a chapbook called *A Serious Morning*.

Byron wrote, "I awoke one morning and found myself famous." Marcus Aurelius, in his *Meditations*, volume 1, said, "In the morning, when thou art sluggish at rousing thee, let this thought be present: 'I am rising to a man's work.'"

The word *morning* is used constantly in the King James Bible, from Genesis to Revelation. In Genesis 1:5, we read, "And God called the light Day, and the darkness he called Night. And the evening and the morning were the first day." In the strange and mysterious book of Revelation, chapter 22, verse 16 says, "I, Jesus, have sent mine angel to testify unto you these things in the churches. I am the root and the offspring of David, and the bright and morning star."

In ancient days, the problems of night were obvious. Animals and robbers abounded, and the metaphorical allusion of night to danger and morning to safety must have begun early in the world's history. And yet morning has its own geography and history as well, a rich but scattered story extending back millennia.

I have always been a "morning person," rising before dawn to exult in the slow growing of the light. Birds that sing and hunt in darkness take to their silences. Suspected shapes of tree and rock assume their daylight outlines, assertive and obvious. But when does morning start? Is dawn when the sun breaks our horizon or when we can first see the world before us? And when is morning over? Noon? At the end of rush hour?

In his delightful 1941 book *The Road of a Naturalist*, Donald Ross Petrie wrote, "The amateur spirit, which is that of doing a thing for the love of it, does not in science differ from the credo of the professional.... Exploration begins at the back fence, and the limits of the field are the ends of the world" (165–66).

In the more than six decades since then, science has become far more reductive, and whole-body disciplines such as botany and zoology have vanished, replaced by intricate cell-level studies. Sometimes the morphology of a complete organism seems less important than the mechanisms of mitochondria.

Morning, which is about science and sociology, about superstition and history, about architecture and the arts, about philosophy and religion, is a subject of great breadth, but one so daunting few have tried to approach it whole, as a zoologist once did a zebra.

It is not my aim to do so in this book, either. And yet morning is, of course, inescapable, even for those who drank champagne until 3:00 A.M. and find the new day is like a dagger in the brain. The subject is massive, which may be why so few books have been written about it. Yet for those of us who love morning, who wait with wonder for the smudge of orange light on the trunk of a white oak, this time of day brings its own magic. Literature, music, and art are full of it. In the Romantic era, morning often "revealed" the "truth" of what happened in the night before—often something terrible and unexpected. Would Poe have ever thought of setting "The Raven" in the morning?

Many of us are creatures of possibility, and the Protestant faith, which in cultural or religious ways pervades American society, makes its case for the new day: "When morning gilds the sky, my heart awakening cries, let Jesus Christ be Lord," goes the old hymn. Religious ecstasy may come in the night, but it's more often associated with light. Morning as a metaphor for hopefulness probably began to change only with the introduction of electric lights.

The English word *morning* itself has been around for about 750 years, perhaps first showing up as *morewening* in

The Owl and the Nightingale around 1250, then in its modern spelling about 1330, formed, according to *Chambers's Encyclopedia of Etymology*, from the Middle English *morn* on the same pattern as *evening*, which preceded it in common usage (678). The flower we call the morning glory wasn't so called until the early nineteenth century, and is of American coinage. An obvious lineage is from the German *morgen*, or the Old English *margen*.

Nature writers from Thoreau and Darwin to E. O. Wilson and Terry Tempest Williams have taken note of morning, but broader questions remain, and I set out to think of morning as an old-fashioned botanist might consider conifers. Though I have been a science writer for more than two decades (as well as a novelist and poet), I am not a scientist and wish to make that clear from the outset. I am not even an especially accomplished naturalist, though I have studied my own 7 acres in the North Georgia woods intensively for more than fifteen years.

What I am is a lover of morning. I enjoy the articulation of the world as light filters into the trees. In *Hamlet*, Shakespeare wrote, "But soft! Methinks I scent the morning air" (act 1, scene 5) and some days I, too, can almost smell the new day rising. We say day*break* and the *crack* of dawn, and neither makes sense to me, whatever their etymology. To me, morning is a gentle transition, almost like the arousal from an old lover.

The owl has gone silent. Sometimes, a whippoorwill will begin its fruity and maddening three-note symphony in the early evening and sing for hours. Our owls are not as persistent, but they are vastly louder. The crows, which have been visiting for days, are starting to sing what sounds to me like *mnaw* outside, too, and a squirrel lies flat and barks at them as they argue over a plate of birdseed my wife Linda has put on the deck below my study.

One might consider that the morning birds and night birds watch the sun and wait for their turn, but it's far more complicated. They respond to so-called circadian rhythms, "physiological processes that occur on a periodic basis... and appear to have some connection to light-dark cycles." Washington University hosts a delightful web site called the MadSci Network, and Dr. Kurt Wallenburg, an associate professor from that university in St. Louis, writes: "These cycles are governed by a set of genes which have a periodic pattern to their expression. Usually, the presence of light will turn on one gene, which in turn activates several other genes. This type of regulation is known as downstream activation" (posted on the site 2/7/01).

So, my owls and crows are not watching for morning, but their actions were *formed* by it. I suppose natural selection created the genes' expression, but now the birds' singing is programmed, like a security light that comes on when darkness arrives. It's intriguing to think that human reactions to morning are also gene driven, but with blinds drawn against the neighbors or streetlights, alarm clocks probably regulate our mornings more than circadian rhythms. Research, as I will point out later, is continuing.

I have been curious all my life why some people love the morning and others despise it. We have morning sickness, which is a good reason for pregnant women to hate getting up. During the night, the many species of bacteria in our mouths go on a reproductive spree, with some doubling their population in twenty minutes. Many break down sulfur-containing compounds and leave an unpleasant taste and smell. So for us, morning also means heading for the toothbrush (MadSci Network, 5/25/2000). On the good side, we weigh a little less in the morning than when we go to bed because we continue to use energy as we sleep while not adding sugar and fat. (If you don't use AC, you can lose weight through perspiration, too.) In general, one rarely finds people who are equivocal about morning. They either love it or hate it.

In my family, I am the only morning lover. I get up to write every day at 4:15 or so and am shaved and showered and have finished my day's writing before I leave for my office at the University of Georgia, where I am a professional science writer. Linda has no use for morning and never has. My two children also sit and stare—in some cases glare—until it's time to leave. (Our son now lives on his own, but when he was in college and living at home, he would sometimes be going to bed as I was getting up.) I have often, in groups, asked a simple question: Morning person or night person? Everyone instantly has an answer and will create an endless riff on the subject like a jazz artist. In my experience, true morning lovers are somewhat like left-handers—exotic remnants of some past necessity.

Perhaps there is an as-yet-undiscovered sentinel gene that forces morning lovers out of bed early and alertly. (Research in 2004 points this way.) I awaken like my dog—I get up, shake once, and I'm completely awake and ready to work. Surely in the dawn of humanity (that metaphor again), there were those who must guard the night and those who must start a family's work in the morning. In Southeastern Indian chiefdoms, cooking and taking care of family life was the work of women, and such was probably true for individuals and societies as humanity developed. If they had to be the first to arise, then one might suspect that a wake-up gene, if there were such a thing, would be selected to appear more in women than men.

Most women I've known, though, are night people. I realize that's anecdotal information and useless, but it's interesting to contemplate. Perhaps these days, at least in America, being a morning person may have a direct relation to how good (or nasty) one's boss is. It's chilling to think that rotten bosses may be acting on natural selection.

I entered "Morning Has Broken" on a popular web search engine, expecting to find a few versions of Eleanor Farejon's much-loved hymn, made popular by Cat Stevens in the seventies. Instead, I got back more than 18,000 hits, including a number of rants against morning. A humorist named Anitra Freeman said she once interviewed a man who said, "If I saw 5 A.M. on the sidewalk, I'd shoot it."

Few people plan their weddings for the morning. This may just be sheer practicality, but I suspect it's more than that. There has long been anecdotal evidence that more people die in the morning, and morning heart attacks are common because the sudden jolt of awakening can often cause a heart made delicate by disease or obstruction to fail entirely.

There are entire liturgies for the morning. Morning was crucial to the early Egyptians, and became intertwined with their religious rituals.

In short, the turning of Earth back toward the sun after hours in darkness, has always been freighted with meanings—good or bad depending on philosophy or religion or whether you lived in a place where lions were on the prowl.

And yet morning seems, to me, completely fascinating. The world changes; some animals go to sleep and others awaken. Light shifts and rituals unfold. Much of the world doesn't even have electricity and welcomes light as humankind always did, with gratitude and hope.

Another day. Overnight, rain has spangled Wildcat Ridge, and this morning, the white oak leaves near my study window are spotted with raindrops. Each green structure seems to hold a thousand glass globes, and the new light of a Friday morning twinkles through them. It is almost summer, and the light is diffused, and the day soon will be hot. It's also Daylight Savings Time, which I have never liked. It seems unnatural and contrived to me, a collective pretense, as it were. Those areas that have refused to go along with the gimmick have my admiration. Of course, if there were truly massive energy shortages or we were in the midst of a global conflict such as World War II, then I could understand it for the energy savings alone. But in the American South, it changes nothing this time of year; air conditioning runs anyway. Lights burn anyway.

I have already taken a walk in the first light of morning. The crows were muttering and the owl, in his final cries for the night, fluffed for sleeping. Shapes appeared, phantom recluses. I found dozens of raccoon tracks along Wildcat Creek, but no raccoons. The humidity, which is always highest in the morning, was thick with messages of rain. I stood in silence and watched the sunrise climb through my woods.

I am thinking of music by the Norwegian composer Edvard Grieg called, of course, "Morning," from his *Peer Gynt Suite*. Generations of piano students have learned it, a gentle evocation that describes day from the first hint of light to the glory of full dawn. Then I remember the "Sunrise" movement from the *Grand Canyon Suite* by Ferde Grofé, a piece better known for its donkey-clopping "On the Trail" movement which was a popular hit decades ago. Artists have always been attracted to the dawn-as-epiphany motif, and I suppose I am, too.

When I was nineteen, my father gave me a little book with excerpts from *Walden*, and I first read there, before I bought the whole book, Thoreau's feelings about morning: "How many mornings, summer and winter, before yet any neighbor was stirring about his business, have I been about mine! I never assisted the sun materially in his rising, but, doubt not, it was of the last importance only to be present at it."

That, too, has been my inheritance and my goal: to assist the sun in rising and spread that majesty on field and city. Walk with me for a while, and let's see if I can help you see my own life and land in the light of morning.

In the Beginning

Dan, my neighbor across the dirt road on which we live, sometimes cuts his field in the middle of the afternoon, wearing only trousers and no shirt. He sweats and glistens, and he seems to love the day's streaming heat, the weight of sunlight. My friend Christine hates the cold and dreams of moving to Hawaii or Puerto Rico, where it is always hot and the cool air has turned into memory.

Give me a cold winter day, though, a lowering sky, and a threat of sleet. Some stray gene has made its way into my makeup that leads me toward the cooler parts of year, of the day. And yet I am a Southerner born and bred, and I was an adult before I ever lived in a house with an air conditioner. I can't decide if one ancestor came from Iceland and loved that country or another came from the equatorial climates and hated those. Either way, I suffer in summer and come back alive when the leaves change.

Each day has its seasons, too, and I have always most coveted the season of morning, with its particular birdcalls, shifting shadows, and gold-orange light brushed along the trunks of oaks.

A while back, Megan, our daughter, who was then eleven, had a bad dream, and the next morning she lay on the sofa, talking it out with her mother. That country was so real, so threatening, that she had trouble finding her way back into this world. Later, they went to the zoo, and Megan forgot the dream, letting it fade into memory.

Because I have serious back trouble, I often awaken in pain, and rising and stretching, pouring a first cup of coffee, is a balm that brings me back toward the light. I have not slept until dawn in years, and often in the darkness of early morning, I walk on to our back deck and look toward the woods I know lie below us toward Wildcat Creek, and I will navigate by sounds that still belong to the night. When moonlight frosts the forest, I can see the familiar shapes: white oaks, hickories, and dogwoods, a huge pine in the flood plain, the now-empty dog pen with its twin igloos, remnants of the time Morgan and Thunder, our two large dogs, were alive. Now Morgan lies buried just beside the pen, and Thunder disappeared one evening and never came home, though I searched for four long days. Honeysuckle and grape vines have rolled over the pen, and no dog bays in the night from that enclosure, whose door is always ajar.

Often, the air at this time of morning is heavy and still, though sometimes a breeze rises and tickles the highest leaves in the canopy. The great Aldo Leopold in *A Sand County Almanac* saw this early air.

A dawn wind stirs on the great marsh, he wrote. With almost imperceptible slowness, it rolls a bank of fog across the wide morass. Like the white ghost of a glacier the mists advance, riding over phalanxes of tamarack, sliding across bog-meadows heavy with dew. A single silence hangs from horizon to horizon.

We don't have "phalanxes of tamarack" on Wildcat Ridge, but this southern edge of the Piedmont has oaks and dogwoods and native azaleas, lavender moss verbena and passionflowers. I once watched the sunrise on a bloodroot (*Sanguinaria Canadensis*), seeing the orange brush of dawn paint those white petals until they seemed cut from peach skins.

Last week I walked into the yard in the pre-dawn darkness. Deep woods surround us, though in winter we can see the houses of our neighbors to the east and west through the heavy stands of pine and oak. A raccoon walked with great wariness through the woods, stopping at times to reconnoiter, to listen. A deer stood statue-still not 100 feet away in the wispy fog that lay like a milk mustache on the soft moss. She watched me, but she was not afraid and so began to twitch an ear and then walk slowly away down the hill, past car-sized granite boulders, toward the creek.

I could see in that moonlight the latest of our Christmas trees, which we bring outside and prop against two oak trees that begin with a single trunk. We put them there and watch the seasons turn them red-brown, strip their needles. Time turns their soft, pliable bristles into dry and crushable things.

A whippoorwill began its three-note solo. Washington Irving in "The Legend of Sleepy Hollow" took the Romantic approach to this bird:

The moon of the whip-poor-will from the hillside; the boding cry of the tree-toad, that harbinger of storm; the dreary hooting of the screech owl.

Someone once counted a whippoorwill singing the same crazy three notes 1,088 times in a row before taking a break (*The Cape Codder*, May 20, 2003). I've looked for one numerous times, bird guide in hand and moving with as much stealth as I can, but I've never *seen* a singing whippoorwill. They call for mates, proclaim territory, getting stuck on those three notes. (Most rock and folk songs from the Sixties used only three chords. I spy a Master's thesis here somewhere.) We rarely see raccoons, either, but each morning that I walk down the slope to

Wildcat Creek, I can find hundreds of their claw-footed tracks in the wet sand.

Tree frogs were getting tired. I knew that first light was not far away, but to the plants and animals of Wildcat Ridge, it was still the season of night, for hunting and staking claims, for becoming predator or prey. Morning is only an idea this long before first light.

In that darkness, I saw a rock near Linda's perennial garden. She loves turtles and collects them in stone and pottery, as garden *objets d'art* and for display around the house. For a moment I thought it was a concrete turtle, but then it moved slightly, and I came close enough to see it was a box tortoise. I backed away and returned long after daylight to find she was still there, squatting over a hole she'd dug to lay eggs.

Megan, Linda, and I came out to watch her work.

"She's been there how long?" Linda asked.

"Since before first light," I said.

"Why here out in the open, though?" Linda asked. Megan wondered the same thing, but I wasn't sure. The garden is full of turtle statuary, but surely some stray tortoise mother didn't confuse this with a gathering place of her kind. Whatever the reason, she stayed in the same position, squatting over the hole she had dug in the red soil, for four hours.

Later, in the heat of the day, I came back to check on her, and she was gone, and her incubation chamber had been covered and patted flat, like mud cakes from a small child.

The next morning, I went back out and waited, but we never found her again. If a line of small waddling turtles ever erupted from that spot, it happened during the night or while we were at work and school.

———

One morning in June, I arose to make my coffee and write. I am habitually sitting at my computer when the first light of day yawns through the forest, which lies below my second-floor study. This morning, I fed our beagle, Murphy, and put the kettle on, when I noticed our black cat, Alaska, sitting on the hearth and looking up the chimney.

We sometimes host swifts in the summer, and their chatty giggle can make our cats revert to their naturally predatory prowling. This morning, though, a quiet rain fell all over north central Georgia, and Alaska—whom we also call Spud in the way that pets can be saddled with half a dozen names or more—sat placidly. I listened but could hear no swifts.

"What's up the chimney?" I asked. I realized as I came close that he was listening to rain on the copper chimney cap two stories up, a soft percussive patter of exquisite delight. I sat next to him and listened while the kettle boiled. He turned on me with his huge green eyes, as if to say, cats, too, listen for sounds that promise no harm.

———

These acres in the early morning darkness are my sinecure and my secular altar. We have rattlesnakes and copperheads along Wildcat Ridge, and once an obviously sick or rabid raccoon came staggering through our yard in the middle of the day. Since I do not own a gun, I called Janine, who lives with her husband Terry and their children in the next house east on the ridge, and told her to tell Terry. Perhaps their kids should stay inside. Terry owns guns. The raccoon disappeared into the woods, however, where it no doubt harmed nothing else and became part of the ridge as it was meant to.

I am not afraid of walking in the woods, though, if I announce my presence with steps noisy enough for warning but quiet enough for aesthetics.

We have lived here fifteen years now, and I have had epiphanies in the pre-dawn, intimations of solitary happiness, which on some days I may call God. This place, where men and women have lived for thousands of years, is mine for a short while, and even when I cannot see it, I am preciously bound to it.

Edwin Way Teale taught me, through his books, how to look at land. He was with *Audubon* magazine for nearly forty years, but his eyes were not honed just for birds. My favorite book of his remains *Autumn in America*, but I'm also deeply fond of *The Lost Woods: Adventures of a Naturalist*. He says there:

In talking to others, I have come to believe that most of us have had some such experience—that some lonely spot, some private nook, some glen or streamside-scene impressed us so deeply that even today its memory recalls the mood of a lost enchantment.

Scientists don't use words like "lost enchantment" in their writing or at scholarly meetings, but I have been astounded, as a science writer for the past twenty-one years, at how many of them think that way. I once interviewed a scientist at length about a paper she had coming out in *Science*, a signal achievement for any researcher. She spoke with passion about the genetic components of the breakthrough, about mitochondrial DNA and alleles. Then I asked a simple question: "When you discovered this, how did you feel?"

She stopped speaking, and for a moment, her mouth hung open in shock at the question, and when she spoke again, her tone had softened.

"Like I'd opened a door into the light," she said. She smiled wistfully for a moment, remembering a time that might never come again. "You're not going to use *that* in the story, are you?"

"No," I said. "I was just wondering." The enchantment remained for her, but already it was slipping into memory, and she did not want to let it go and so had fashioned a metaphor to shape it in her mind.

An archaeologist I know once opened a tomb in Carthage and saw marvelous artifacts. Remembering Howard Carter's words on first looking into Tutankhamen's tomb in 1922, that he saw "wonderful things," I asked her if she said the same words. She turned and smiled at me, not at all expecting the question.

"I did," she said with a shy grin. "I sure did."

I have often wondered if there is a difference, to the creatures and plants of our acres, in the darkness at midnight and that just before sunrise. Common sense, on which I rely far more than anyone with common sense would, tells me they understand the difference. Raccoons and whippoorwills know the time is coming to take cover and sleep. Deer become more wary. Foxes and coyotes—we have both, if not in profusion—cock an eye toward the east.

Plants are light sensitive, too. Morning glories fold up like origami when the heat of day swells over them, while other blossoms open into the light. In the burrowing winter chill of our cove, where it is typically 7 to 10 degrees cooler than it is in Atlanta, ferns stay knotted in the soil beneath their dead fronds, alive and waiting for longer light, greater warmth.

One morning more than twenty years ago, I awoke where we lived in Athens and went into our living room, feeling the weight of some impenetrable dread. We lived at the edge of a small forest then, too, though the entire area is now defaced with condos and crowded housing.

Light was just coming up, and I should have been in my study writing, making the same mistakes over and over as I learned to shape a phrase, but this morning, something felt broken in me, and I sat with my coffee and looked out the picture window across our lawn toward the home of our English professor friend, Charles.

I am addicted to classical music, and I don't use the word *addicted* lightly. If I cannot have it every day, I feel strangled by the world. This morning, in pre-CD days, I put on a record of Samuel Barber's *Adagio for Strings*, a piece that has become a chestnut through overplaying and use in films like *Platoon* and *The Elephant Man*. It is invariably associated with sorrow and death and was played over the radio when Franklin Roosevelt and John Kennedy died.

My hands trembled. I did not know what was going on, but I sat silently as the sun rose through the Japanese maple in our front yard, sat as Charles's house took shape, from the flat perspective of a streetlight to the three dimensions of dawn.

I went to work as always that day and did not find out until later that night that my Uncle Dave, a man I was deeply fond of, had died almost at the very moment I played Barber's *Adagio*. There seems no rational way that I could have known that such a thing happened, and though I knew he was ill, I had no idea he was dying.

I have spoken to many others who have had almost identical experiences, and many of them have happened at that hour, and to some, the pre-dawn takes on a disturbing aura. If night allows us to forget, day makes clear our most common dreads. But if there is a rattlesnake on the path to our creek, at least I can see and avoid it. The mind has equal claims on clarity and mystery, it seems.

As a science writer, I have learned to stay close to facts, to doubt, to inquire, to know my subjects. Therefore I have studied science almost daily for more than two decades, realizing that while I have an immense aptitude for curiosity, I have far less for the scientific method.

The scientists I admire most are ones who are brilliant researchers who have kept open that channel to connections and even mysteries, to rigor and beauty. E. O. Wilson is such a man, and the day I shook his hand was deeply special to me. My friend John Avise, formerly a genetics professor at the University of Georgia and a marvelous stylist in his many books, is a world-class evolutionary biologist. He sees that larger picture with affection and the eyes of a boy collecting wildflowers.

I want to believe in the primacy of science, but I am inevitably drawn back to the sound of rain on the copper cap of a chimney. Even if I cannot see that part of morning, I know it is there, and I believe.

The Shape of Dawn: The Day's First Sun

The sky appeared slate-gray through the canopy of oaks this morning, laden with humidity and speaking of July, which will arrive in a few days. I walked into the woods and stood ankle deep in leaf litter and deadfall and listened. Crows spoke solemnly, not raising their voices. A pileated woodpecker banged with desultory intentions against the trunk of a dead white oak, bagging bugs. A male cardinal watched me, Audubon-still upon the long branch of a tulip poplar.

I have often wondered why I moved to the woods. I did not do it to make a point or to live simply like Thoreau. I hold no brief for physical discomfort, nor do I abhor all Western civilization and want to "get back to nature." Our home has central heat and air, and my study is carpeted, lined with bookcases like an English gentleman's den. We have not camped in years, though I keep planning to start again soon, despite my degenerating spinal discs.

Part of this move was to escape the sounds of the city. I grew up on a dirt road, and I live on one now, a place where the predominant noises are those from a freshening wind and red-tail hawks. Their high shriek edges me with the kind of wild joy that eighteenth-century poets and naturalists described with a dumbfounded ecstasy.

And yet I think I'm being honest when I say I don't go toward the natural world looking for poetry or spirituality. Somehow, though, the world of these steep hills, these huge exposed boulders, of Wildcat Creek, takes me inward, and I am helpless to prevent it.

Sometimes, nature comes inside. It is the last Monday in June as I write this, and a few moments ago, not long after five and well before dawn, I felt something crawling on my foot. I backed up sharply, thinking it might be a scorpion—they sometimes creep into the house, and one stung our son Brandon a few years back. On my foot was what looked like a small beetle, and it clung there, suddenly flashing a cool fire. We Southerners call them lightning bugs, though "firefly" seems a more elegant word in all. I scooped it off my foot and held it for a moment, and its wings fluttered a greeting as it spun cool light in my palm. I took it outside and opened my hand, and its wings shuddered for a moment, and it lit up in what seemed like delight then flew outward into the dark yard.

No wonder we incline to metaphor.

We own just under 7 acres of land 7 miles south of Watkinsville, Georgia, a town of only a few hundred people. While our house and the dirt road on which we live would seem isolated to an urban dweller, it's an easy drive to Athens and the University of Georgia, where I have worked for more than two decades.

Except for a small yard and garden spot carved out of the plot, our land is all bearded with woods, though for a century it was cotton country and thereafter cattle pasture. When I stand in the forest just before dawn and watch its daily light-painting begin, I know why I moved here. The land retains its memory, metaphorically at least: rusted strands of barbed wire with large gaps run through the woods, tree to tree, like an ill-sutured scar. Cattle once spilled down these hills. But when I come here for first light, cattle are only the stuff of imagination. We have not cut the wire, because it somehow speaks of another past, just as do the potsherds that wash up in the creek. There are many pasts in each square foot of earth, but people usually ignore them.

In a climax hardwood forest at dawn, the present is very often enough. Each spring, I come down to watch the early light baste trilliums.

The sessile trillium is a perennial and one of sixteen species of trilliums with sessile flowers. (*Sessile* is a lovely word referring to stalkless structures—this trillium sits magnificently atop a single stem in rich forests.) The leaves are two shades of green, a fine pale and a much darker shade that is mottled differently from plant to plant. Its subtle purple flower begins as a tightly held bud that relaxes as the season moves among its days and nights.

When we first moved to Wildcat Ridge, a friend came out to walk the land and took one look at the hundreds of trilliums spread down the sharp slope and almost gasped.

"Do you know what people pay for these things in a nursery?" he asked.

"Not really."

"You could sell these things for a fortune."

But they are the forest's fortune, I wanted to reply. I have often knelt in the leaf litter to watch the first light butter the leaves of a trillium.

Megan has discovered a Turk's-cap lily growing next to our propane tank. The use of gas fire logs embarrasses me, but with my bad back, lugging firewood is a serious problem for me. I feel myself slumping, even shortening, and I do not want to hasten it with an armload of seasoned oak on sleety January evenings.

"That's incredible," I say. Linda comes, and we gather around it, amazed that the seed has germinated in the edge of the woods where the lily's almost brazen pride is obvious to everyone. The stalk is huge—they can grow to 3 meters—and numerous bell-shaped flowers hang upside-down from the stems. My *Wildflowers of the Southeastern United States* (by Wilbur Duncan and Leonard Foote), which has been my almost daily guide for twenty-five years, speaks as always with pure poetry: "The leaves chiefly whorled, the blades with smooth margin and usually widest at the middle. Flowers nodding, as many as 65, but more often 25 or less." Flowers *nodding*. What lovely nomenclature.

All we know is they are bright pumpkin orange, dazzling and wind-stirred, and we can't stop looking at them.

So, the day after we found them, I came out, not at first light, but at *first sun*, and there is a profound difference.

I love the pre-dawn stirring, the density of air, the retreat of animals, in Henry Beston's words, "to whom the night gives power." But those first pale yellow shafts of first sun never fail to move me, and there is something profoundly primal about the appearance of sun above the eastern horizon.

I sat in the moss near the Turk's-cap and watched, silently gauging when the sunlight would breach the tree line. My beagle Murphy sat with me in wonder. She did not ask what I planned, why I was there. She simply held to my side, waiting not on light but on my movement or my words. We were not 15 feet from the spot where the turtle had laid her eggs at the edge of Linda's perennial garden.

It came with the slow suddenness of revelation: A tiny breeze, a slash of sun, and the lilies began to nod. I felt somehow *convinced*, that this was a demonstration of stamen, pistil, corolla, calyx, spun into motion by light and the stirring of air masses that once belonged in Alaska or even Siberia. In this sun, I could see the leaves were more than "chiefly whorled"—they bobbed in their dazzling yards. If I were a bee, I would be homing in, without delay, for all the pollen I could bear away.

Homer spoke of "rosy-fingered" dawn, and, sometimes, cloud structures and seasonal changes spread that rose color over North Georgia. But I have noticed lilac more often, even a richer vermilion.

Often a mist or fog brings morning in a damp sheet, and then morning is half gone before the sun yawns through the gray-white. I understand the history of visions better in this kind of light.

A few days ago, I was driving to work very early in the morning, thinking of a dozen problems in my life, each with a difficult if not impenetrable solution. There were no cars on Oliver Bridge Road, the stretch of country lane that meanders through horse country back toward Athens. A large forest of planted pines once huddled up to the roadside, but a few years back, the owner dramatically thinned them, though at least he didn't clear-cut the acreage. Now, the under-story is returning, brambles and yearling hardwoods, and the sun sometimes throws Spartan spears through the canopy, all drama and pride.

This morning, though, a many-layered fog lay across the woods, finding its own wet levels according to topography and wind currents. I came just past the forest where it turns from near-wilderness to a neighbor's enormous yard, and there, standing statue-still in the mist, was a twelve-point buck. Deer, of course, are common here—and everywhere else now it seems. We spent one entire summer watching a doe in our yard trailed by two spotted fawns, and often I speak in a slow, high-pitched voice to show them I mean no harm. But this buck was more than sheer magnificence. There was a mythic quality to its grandeur, something from E.T.A. Hoffman. I let my car slow to a stop, and still the deer did not move or seem even to exhale.

Thomas Merton in *Raids on the Unspeakable* said, "There is no clock that can measure the speech of this rain that falls all night on the drowned and lovely forest." Just so, there is no memory of first light or first sun that prepares the casual commuter for such a vision, as if the forest had sighed and a stag appeared.

I felt myself suddenly crying, and I was as far from sorrow as I was from the stars. I sat above the idling engine, hearing the raindrop plot of tears in my lap, and for long moments, a palpable lingering, the deer still stood, foursquare, posing. Then, with a strong kick born of muscle and escape, it was gone—as if it had sublimated, gone straight from solid to gas without first turning liquid.

Not a smudge of sunlight burned through the fog, and the pines nearby still dripped the storm from the evening before. I was no longer on a North Georgia roadside at that moment, but in the province of poetry.

When I think of my favorite nineteenth-century nature writers—Thoreau, Burroughs, Muir—I realize that they saw the world with new eyes. They told of wilderness because white men had not tramped those grounds, filtering geology, flora, and fauna through the lens of European pasts.

I believe they must have loved sunrise with the intensity that Albert Bierstadt painted Rocky Mountain sunsets—in a wild rush of discovery. It may seem facile to say that morning across America is pretty much the same everywhere, but that similarity is only bark-deep.

I have seen glorious sunrises in midtown Manhattan and even in the smog-bound skies over Los Angeles. I once sat near my family's campsite near the crest of Mount Mitchell, the peak in North Carolina that is the highest point east of the Rockies, awaiting in the pure dark a glimpse of light. When it came, borne on 45 degrees Fahrenheit in mid-July, I saw the world made anew, dew-damp with mountain laurel and rhododendron. The peace I felt smoothed all the rough joints of my life, mated the days that seemed to bear no matching parts. Scientists turn away from such words, but they see it as I did, and I know they believe.

I have stood ankle deep in a rushing stream in the Colorado Rockies and watched first sun claim fractured, jutting peaks that have caught bighorn sheep like lint on a sweater. And I have waited dozens of times on Eastern seashores to see the molten sun shinning up, perhaps, from memories of Troy.

For years now, whenever I feel the world's meretricious days settling over me like a film of grease, I have re-read Wallace Stegner's "Wilderness Letter," which was published in his great book *The Sound of Mountain Water*. The letter was real, written to one David Pesonen at the Wildland Research Center at UC-Berkeley, an agency that then (1960) was studying wilderness preservation. In Stegner's immortal words,

"Something will have gone out of us as a people if we ever let the remaining wilderness be destroyed.... [A]n American is a civilized man who has renewed himself in the wild."

To me, our approach to morning begins in something far more primal than circadian rhythms or a coughing fit and horror at another day in the office. If there is such a thing as seasonal affective disorder, then there must also be a daylight affective disorder as well. I feel sorrow for those who cannot link Stegner's plea for wilderness with an equal understanding of light in the wilderness.

Another summer morning: I am standing at first sun in our front yard, watching the eastern tiger swallowtails unfold. We have had an abundance this year, and I watch them often, their wings pressed like praying hands, atop a slow inquisitive body. In the morning, they are sluggish, letting the dew evaporate from their wings. They sip nectar off Linda's butterfly bush and other wildflowers.

Sometimes we see monarchs on Wildcat Ridge, but in our fifteen years here, they have been surprise visitors, in transit, spending a few moments flitting among the boughs before disappearing north or south. Each year, when the adult swallowtails come, they bring their own Mardi Gras to the slopes and the creek. I have watched them with delight.

While early mornings are not the best time to study swallowtails, the late afternoon can bring manifold delights. Though this is a book about morning, allow me to digress briefly to speak of one such swallowtail afternoon.

It is after five on an August Friday, and I am standing in the clear rushing shallows of Wildcat Creek. This bracing stream, above which huge boulders rest, sentinels of my Eden, has been on maps for well more than a century. This spring, we have swum through the drama of unceasing rains, and in early July, the creek flooded, turning from a foot-deep and 20-foot-wide stream into a turgid, muddy pond in which the water barely moved—10 feet deep and 40 yards across. When the rains stopped and Wildcat Creek subsided, a layer of fetid mud 18 inches thick caked the channel.

Now, though, the mud has been washed away, and once more the creek is shining, sparkling. Murphy and I have come down to look for stones and artifacts, and already I have found an enormous amethyst crystal, pale purple and perfect, and a rim-sherd from a clay pot made on this land more than a thousand years ago.

I walk east down the creek, taking the ninety-degree curve onto the property of my neighbors Terry and Janine. I have decided to lift my eyes to the soft light of a summer afternoon when I see, like a calendar painting, more than two dozen swallowtails, flitting and hovering, so ungainly in the air that I cannot understand how they achieve lift.

"Oh my God," I say out loud. Murphy, high on the bank above, scouting some wayward scent, turns to look at me. The air seems filled with wings, like the confetti that welcomed Lindbergh home from Paris. I feel as if I had once, perhaps in dreams, visited Paradise, and I have turned this loop in the creek and found it once more. I come forward, wading, my feet dripping sunlight and water with each step, and the butterflies appear to surround me, inquisitive, inviting.

On a huge sandbar stretching along the eastern bank of Wildcat Creek, I see about fifteen of these yellow and black marvels in a heap, engaged in the behavior called "puddling," during which a butterfly sips nutrients with its proboscis. Because they eat only nectar, they need other salts and minerals, and they often get them by settling on a spot where some chance of nature has concentrated the salts they need. Skippers and fritillaries do this, too.

I cannot decide how to look at them. J.A. Baker wrote in his magisterial book *The Peregrine* that he came late to the love of birds and that for years he saw them "only as a tremor at the edge of vision." Just so, I cannot focus now, so I decide to stand in the sunlight for a minute or two, my arms out as if I, too, am a creature of flight. The swallowtails honor me in this posture, coming close as a dream. At such moments I know I am a poor amateur naturalist, for I succumb to *feeling* the moment instead of examining it.

Such ecstasies cannot last, so I reluctantly fold my wings and walk slowly to the scene of their puddling. They let me come close, then closer, and finally so near that I reach out, out, out—so close I could cup the whole bunch in my hand. That must be a powerful place, I think, the kind of land humans in another era would have called magic or holy. Finally, they blow upward off the spot, which is whitish, perhaps from a passing crow. One butterfly, however, will not be cowed, and he remains for the others, like a finger to mark a book page when the phone rings. I reach farther and farther into the late light and finally brush my index finger along the tall country of his folded wings, and he does not move or shudder.

When I back away, walk into the creek's mid-channel, the others return quickly, puddle up once more. All I can think is that this moment of grace has ennobled me, given me secrets that I will carry back to the "civilized" world. It does not escape my notice that this has happened not at *first* sun but very near *last* sun, and that in the animal kingdom, the angle of light and the burden of humidity may mean more than the "time of day."

In some places of light, everything seems to have wings.

That animal kingdom stirs in these woods all night. In high summer, the forest is nearly deafening with a raucous ensemble of cicadas and tree frogs. Someone once wrote that cicadas sound like a buzz saw cutting through metal, and that's about right. Often I find dead cicadas on my paths, wings folded, looking for all the world like just-crushed cigar butts, stubby and unremarkable. Owls demand homage. Coyotes mourn mates, seek bone and sinew for feasts. Mosquitoes roam, hunting a blood meal, feeling for heated mammals. I have been in the forest when the racket was worse than traffic in Times Square—cicadas, owls, night birds, unseen raccoons and opossums, cautious deer. Dogs bark across the creek, their domesticated noise taking on a feral edge in darkness.

Toward morning, that cacophony, as vast and impenetrable as a Charles Ives symphony, begins to fade. The air is its most humid for the day, and heaviness hangs with the coming light. Peacefulness spreads down the sharp slope toward Wildcat Creek. Something has surely been achieved—mating, feeding, the staking of territory, the inevitable death that each living thing bears from the moment of birth.

Because I am not a creature of the night, I must force myself into that kingdom. Morning is my sanctuary, and from first light to first sun, I am a creature born upward into exaltation.

Morning's First Sense: Seeing

I stand on our dirt road in the just-light of a Saturday morning, and Murphy has crossed over into Dan's field, disappeared through the line of tree trunks into his woods. I am trying to shut down everything but sight, to see as an artist sees, as Van Gogh saw stars and wheat fields, as Cezanne saw apples and pears, as Michelangelo saw God. Of course I cannot, for such sight is a gift. My gifts are my family and this land, but I can strain toward even those gifts I do not possess.

As morning matures, so do the lines, shapes, and colors of the coming day. When first light turns up its wick in the east, I mark the world in black and gray, two-dimensional, almost unknowable. There is no wind, and summer still holds its day length over this land, though the blackberries have long gone, and the acute angles of Canada geese no longer jab south.

What can I see? Shapes, not systems. A crescent moon is setting at the high point of a gone-wild hill at the end of Dan's field, and that hill is studded with low persimmon trees, clots of broom sedge. Then intimations of leaf and limb, grass blades, stones in the road. And—blessings—color.

Each day not only brings first light and first sun, but *first color*. An increasingly small percentage of Americans live deep in the country as we do, and urban dwellers miss this abundance. I cannot imagine again being away from it, and now, as the day comes, I seem to *hear* the colors, greens like the string section of an orchestra, siennas and umbers like massed horns. Great streaks of gray roll through the woods along the reach of limbs, and the sky is pale violet and slate.

What part of this is the seen, and what part of it is me, the watcher of it? In one of his notebooks from around 1960, Loren Eisley, one of the first naturalists I read as a teenager, wrote, "A wilderness exists in man which refuses to be studied." This surely must apply to the meaning of first color each morning, which seems simple enough.

The visible spectrum is part color, part illumination. The colors have gone nowhere, of course, so we tend to supplement their black-gray-green with memory. We enrich some details, slight others, but we rarely watch the world coming back to itself in the morning the way photographers once watched images appear on prints in a developing bath.

If my retired neighbors, Lawrence and Virginia, came riding toward town on the dirt road just before first color, I would see the dragon headlights of their truck, but little more. What we see in morning changes rapidly but with great subtlety, and the world comes back in the Grumbacher red of a male cardinal or the black angle of a drifting turkey vulture. If I hear a pair of mourning doves speaking from tree to tree, that does not mean I can yet see their glove-gray curves.

As light lifts like an impossible theatrical curtain east toward where my brother Mark and his family live on another dirt road, the few visible stars retreat, duty done. Then I see them, staked to Dan's field in a gorgeous silence: the doe and her twin fawns, watching me, alert and inquisitive, certain of no harm but unable to act upon that thought.

At first, they appear almost black, like charcoal outlines in a book of nature identification, but soon their raw sienna paints itself on their flanks. The ivory spots that speckle the fawns come out like constellations. And their eyes are brown, what I see in the mirror each day, but much more alert, purposeful, and unknowing. The doe's right ear flops toward something I cannot hear. She listens for all of them. I take on first color for them, too, and I am bipedal, something to steer around.

Perspective begins to assert its primacy. Dan's field, neatly mowed as always, has a green depth now, stretching back toward his woods. Murphy sits beside me, a threat to no living thing, a timid dog withal, like some country lady who wears a bonnet to cover her face, a kind but fleeing sort. The dark green of pine needles accepts a softer color with the light. Our road is deer-colored, studded with gravel the color of beech trunks.

To me, afternoon is the country of sun-blasted color, when objects—or their effect on my retinas at least—lose the integrity of their tint, wander toward that pre-dawn flatness morning files away. Of course, this business of first color depends on the weather, cloud cover, rainfall. But afternoon is a dead time, and from one until perhaps six in the Southern summertime, I lose interest.

The deer walk away like a horse and her foals, unhurried, barn-bound. She raises her foot-high white tail in greeting or as a soft warning, and as the sun strikes it, I can see its true color, fine as bone. Hemingway was roaming in metaphor when he spoke of things "true at first light," but I want them to be literal.

I have wondered often if I confuse morning with innocence, with childhood, with a fear of death. Well past fifty now, I think that isn't the case. In *Paradise Regained*, Milton, who experienced the seasons of the day without sight, wrote, "The childhood shows the man/ As morning shows the day." That is true, I think, but I want to shy from the land of metaphor and simile. I want to hold a mirror back up to morning so it can judge for itself when first color comes.

But that is foolish and poetic, too, and shirks the duty of one who wishes to know morning, to understand that a deer's eyes look back him, whether in mirrors or still waters.

Murphy has disappeared over in Dan's woods, following her nose, as beagles will. Once, on a late summer morning, she was inside on her bed by the television long after I had come down to Wildcat Creek to look for driftwood and potsherds. She asked to be let out, not knowing where I was, and Linda opened the door, and Murphy promptly scented my passage and arrived at the creek for me.

A more perfect solitude. In the gospel of Mark, Jesus graced this time of day: "And in the morning, rising up a great while before day, he went out and departed into a solitary place and there prayed."

I am grateful for this time of first color, and if giving thanks is a form of prayer, then I have come into this early morning as a true pilgrim.

Morning and the Rhythms of Daily Life

The science library at the University of Georgia was crowded on an early spring day in 1996, students studying intensely, faculty members rushed and rushing. There are extraordinary riches in those walls on the school's South Campus, with thousands of books on almost any scientific subject. One of my jobs is to interview scientists about their research, write about it, and then try to interest the national and international media to take notice. It was in this capacity that I was reading *Science* that day.

There is a kind of secular holiness about two peer-reviewed journals: *Science* in the United States and *Nature* in England. If you want to know the world's best current science, that is where you start. Trying to keep up, I was scanning research results when I stumbled on something that intrigued me.

Scientists from Rockefeller University and the Howard Hughes Medical Institute had discovered that light sets an organism's rhythms by removing a key protein needed for the body's clock. In the way splendid research always overtakes me, I began to lose sight of the bustle around me and sink into the world of ideas.

Marion Glick, a science writer at Rockefeller just as I am at UGA, said it succinctly in her press release: "The findings, from fruit fly studies, may help explain light's effect on the daily cycle that influences sleep, mental alertness, pain sensitivity, and temperature and hormone levels."

This was a study that immediately caught my attention. Why are some of us morning persons? Why would some people "shoot 5:00 A.M." if they saw it on a sidewalk? The underlying reasons lie in the mysteries of circadian rhythms.

The whole business of understanding biological rhythms isn't especially new. The International Society for Chronobiology was founded in 1937, for example. In the past decade, however, the study of the internal clocks of plants and animals has suddenly become hot.

Many universities are studying biological timing. The *Journal of Circadian Rhythms*, the only open-access online journal in the field, publishes research on rhythms in living organisms and is edited out of the University of South Carolina. There are hundreds of research projects on biological clocks: biological rhythms and aging; interaction of the body clock with cell cycles; how genes regulate these rhythms; how these clocks affect sleep apnea, seasonal affective disorder, and even hypertension.

Morning person? Night person? Scientists are finding out that it isn't a matter just of choice or habit—it looks increasingly likely that we are born to the breed.

(A couple of years after this study was published, I would find myself working in an office connected to a lab where fruit fly research took place. Occasional rogues from the lab buzzed through my office, often landing on my computer monitor for a look at my writing.)

The principal scientist on the Rockefeller study, Michael W. Young, pointed out that animals usually adjust their intrinsic circadian cycles, which can range from about twenty-three to twenty-five hours, to the twenty-four-hour solar day. The molecular key his team discovered lies in two proteins called PER and TIM. (When we think of Linnaeus and all his Latin polysyllables, it comes as something of a shock to see how taciturn modern scientists can be.) These names aren't even acronyms—they are simple abbreviations for "period" and "timeless." All cells in the fruit fly have these proteins, but the cells in the brain are the ones that turn the body clock on and off. As Glick explained, the TIM and PER proteins accumulate in the nuclei of eye cells sensitive to light—photoreceptors—as well as in "pacemaker" cells in the central brain. (PER was discovered at Cal Tech in 1971, but TIM wasn't known until 1994.)

"The molecular mechanisms of PER were not discovered until 1992," Dr. Roberto Refinitti, editor of *The Journal of Circadian Rhythms*, told me.

The process of these proteins in the fruit fly is fascinating, and they are the slaves of light. "Fruit flies raised in total darkness maintain an activity rhythm of about 23.5 hours, but a brief period in light can either delay or advance the cycle," Glick wrote.

Since fruit fly studies often pinpoint similar systems in humans, it's clear the complexity of our relationship to morning and night is extremely knotty and part of our inherited biology.

This was only part of the story, however. A couple of years later, other researchers found what was trumpeted as the "molecular missing link" between sunlight and the circadian clocks in fruit flies and mammals. Another article in *Science*, this one featuring work of Aziz Sancar of the University of North Carolina School of Medicine and Joseph Takahashi of the Howard Hughes Medical Institute (HHMI), found "a new biochemical pathway that senses blue light and thereby connects the sun to the molecular components of the circadian clock," according to an HHMI press release.

As the *Science* story pointed out, the research focused on light-reactive proteins called cryptochromes that are found in the eye and in plants. The two proteins, called Cryptochrome 1 and 2, were first discovered in plants and trigger plant growth as they respond to light in the blue-to-ultraviolet part of the light spectrum. Another article in the same issue of *Science* reported similar success in understanding the issue. (While these proteins were first discovered in the eye, they were later also found in the brain and are believed to be central components of the clock, says Refinitti.)

"In mammals, melanopsin, not a cryptochrome, is considered to be a photopigment," he said.

Morning person? Night person? As with all science, it comes down to genes.

The word "circadian" means "about a day." But the whole biological clock idea has one great curiosity: If it is triggered and affected by light, why does it not coincide directly with the twenty-four-hour solar day? One would think that natural selection would have pointed all living organisms that way over hundreds of thousands of generations.

Instead, these clocks range from perhaps twenty-two to twenty-eight hours. Dr. Hiroaki Daido of the Kyushu Institute of Technology in Japan wondered the same thing, and his study, published in *Physical Review Letters* in July 2001, gave some insights into the problem.

According to the *AIP Bulletin of Physics News*, Daido "devised a mathematical model that explores the competition between species with body clocks of different periods." He first assumed two things: a species' population growth rate depends on the time difference between its body clock period and the twenty-four-hour day; and the "amount of competition between pairs or species becomes more severe with a smaller time difference between their body clocks."

These seem like reasonable assumptions, given that it affects which creatures are nocturnal and which species are looking for food twelve hours apart.

Daido's model demonstrated that the greatest competition occurs in species with twenty-four-hour body clocks, and, thus, having a rhythm in sync with the solar day is a decided *disadvantage* for species due, perhaps, to competition.

When I read of this study, I began to glimpse the evolutionary reasoning behind morning and night people. Genetically, I suppose, subtle differences may have been selected over millennia to smooth competition for food sources or even for territory or mates.

While Daido says that his model also can examine longer time periods such as "circannual rhythms," which control hibernation, among other things, he notes, intriguingly, that natural disasters may have contributed to existing circadian rhythms. If the asteroid theory of dinosaur extinction is anywhere near correct, one can only agree with a shudder.

—————

The real reason someone is a morning or night person, however, may be due to something called the "intrinsic period" of the circadian timing system. Harvard researchers in 2001 published a paper about it in *Behavioral Neuroscience*.

Our tendency has always been to assume that the whole morning-person/night-person dichotomy is a kind of personality trait. Morning people, like Benjamin Franklin, are "healthy, wealthy, and wise." On the other hand, the story goes, night people have more fun.

Senior author of the study, Charles A. Czeisler, said that "While some have argued that extremes in sleep-wake timing are personality characteristics, this study reveals" a biological basis. He goes on to say that "we found that differences in a fundamental property of the circadian timing system, its intrinsic period, will determine whether someone is an early bird, who awakes before dawn or a night owl, who tends to stay up at night but sleeps in late."

Without delving too deeply into the biology, however, I have to wonder: if the intrinsic period of the circadian cycle controls whether we are morning people or night owls, what controls the intrinsic period? Genes, no doubt, and with the dramatic advances in genetics in the past decade, it's only a matter of time before we know the entire mechanism.

Other intriguing aspects of the circadian clock are being uncovered, too. Seasonal affective disorder is, according to the National Mental Health Association, "a mood disorder associated with depression episodes and related to seasonal variations of light." We all know people who get the blues in winter. (Is there a summer seasonal affective disorder? I think I have it.) It's worth quoting from the NMHA web site:

"SAD was first noted before 1845, but was not officially named until the early 1980s. As sunlight has affected the seasonal activities of animals (i.e., reproductive cycles and hibernation), SAD may be an effect of this seasonal light variation in humans. As seasons change, there is a shift in our 'biological internal clocks' or circadian rhythm, due partly to these changes in sunlight patterns. This can cause our biological clocks to be out of "step" with our daily schedules. The most difficult months for SAD sufferers are January and February, and younger persons and women are at higher risk."

So, in many areas of health and life, the clocks keep ticking.

While new advances in genetics and in technology are shedding light on biological rhythms, and the science of chronobiology has only been around for a few decades, people have know about biological rhythms for centuries.

A web site called MoonXscape says it succinctly:

"For more than 2000 years, the rhythmic nature of certain biological patterns has been observed. Aristotle observed the swelling of the ovaries of the sea urchins at full moon; Hippocrates noted daily (24-hour) fluctuations of his patients' symptoms; and Herophilus of Alexandria observed daily changes in pulse rates."

Yet, as far as I can tell, there has been relatively little research specifically directed at morning itself.

By late 2002, a light-sensitive protein in the eye called melanopsin was taking center stage in the study of the regulation of circadian rhythms. Research published in *Science* asserted that mice lacking the gene for melanopsin "show a dramatic deficiency in their ability to regulate circadian rhythms by light," according to a story by Jules Asher at the National Institutes of Mental Health, which partially funded the work.

The researchers used a so-called "knockout-mouse"— a lab creature bred to lack a specific gene. Another study in the same issue of *Science* also implicated melanopsin. Asher's story is the best yet I've seen on the nature of circadian rhythms:

"Each day, a clock in the brain's hypothalamus that governs daily rhythms—sleeping/waking, body temperature, eating, arousal—is reset by light detected in the eyes. Yet how this works has been a mystery. Light can still reset the clock even if the rods and cones, the photoreceptors in the retina for vision, are removed, but not if the eyes are removed. Hence, scientists have hypothesized that the eyes must contain a system of photoreceptors for resetting the clock that is separate from the system of sight."

It turns out that nerve cells in the retina contain melanopsin—something that only became clear in 2002. Most of these cells involve vision, but a tiny fraction do other jobs, including regulate the body clock, which is in the suprachiasmatic nucleus of the hypothalamus. Just how it all works remains unclear, but the researchers proposed that "other mechanisms for light input play a role." It has been known for a while that in plants and fruit flies, for example, according to the paper, "independent photoreceptors with overlapping roles may function to adapt the organism to the natural changes in light quality and irradiance."

In fact, PER and TIM aren't the only proteins involved with setting the body clock, either. In *Drosophilia* (the fruit fly), there are actually six well-understood proteins that play a role: PER and TIM, along with CLOCK, CYCLE, DOUBLE-TIME, and CRYPTO-CHROME.

Since I've written these words, dozens of research projects all over the world are pushing the boundaries of ignorance in body clocks rapidly backward.

———

So, to state it simply, natural clocks bind the living world. A fungus called *Neurospora crassa* has been studied a great deal, and its light-regulated genes, according to the web site Allsciencestuff.com "also control carotenoid (photo-protective pigments) synthesis, spore formation, photo-adaption, and phototropism (growth toward a light source.)"

As a delightful site called whyfiles.org points out, "…sunlight is just one distinction between day and night. Some animals, like horses, hares, and humans, are active during days—even cloudy ones—while mice, raccoons, and skunks prefer skulking in moonlight and starlight. Plants churn out more chlorophyll during daytime. Even in a lowly blue-green alga, cell division, nitrogen fixation, photosynthesis, and respiration all reflect time of day or night."

It's no wonder that jetting off to China turns the body clock upside down.

I take all this—and there are thousands of articles and reliable websites online, not to mention the periodical section of any good science library to consult—that the whole issue of morning is something far beyond tradition and fatigue. If having farmers for ancestors naturally selected us to be early risers, then many of my friends who hate morning more than the flu haven't heard it yet. Their ancestors must have been nightclub owners.

My wife and daughter tend to growl upon first awakening, too. One thing I have found—and I don't know the genetic basis for it—is that night people had rather take a beating than listen to the early, cheery greetings of a born morning person.

The Morning of a New World

I crave a more perfect solitude in part because I despise crowded places. I grew up in the woods of north central Georgia, often alone, and though I have dear friends and a loving extended family, I am happiest in the deep woods of Wildcat Ridge.

For reasons that now escape me, I spent many years as a newspaper editor, overseeing a daily madness that included high-strung, but very talented, writers and artists. The work appealed, I believe, not to my need to inform and persuade, but to an innate belief that order can be imposed on chaotic systems. This, of course, is among the great follies of the ages, but you haven't learned that when you're twenty-two. This urge is also the reason I have embraced spirituality for most of my life.

Christians, Jews, Buddhists, Moslems, Hindus, and all manner of other believers and religions have a special relationship with morning. I do not propose to present a survey of ideas and practices, but it's interesting to note that in the Bible there are, by my count, 214 uses of the word *morning*. In truth, I thought there would have been more, but what really surprised me is that 197 of those instances are in the Old Testament. The New Testament is far shorter, of course, but it has only seventeen instances of *morning*.

Can you guess which book of the Old Testament uses *morning* the most? A cinch—Genesis, right? Well, Genesis uses the word a great deal—nineteen times, more than the entire New Testament. But the real surprise to me is Exodus, in which the word appears an amazing thirty-two times. The story of Moses and the Children of Israel absolutely sparkles with morning—and often, great things are in the air.

Moses paid particular attention to the morning, which serves both as a literal time of day and a great metaphor for the beginnings of a "chosen people." In Exodus 24:4, we read (from the King James Version): "And Moses wrote all the words of the Lord, and rose up early in the morning, and builded an altar under the hill, and twelve pillars, according to the twelve tribes of Israel."

From reading Exodus, one can only conclude that Moses was the quintessential morning person, and that he was forever making the Children of Israel rise early and get on with things. Of course, we don't know if it was dawn, but it *was* morning. Biblical reasons aside, no wonder Moses went up Mt. Sinai alone: everyone else was probably sleeping in.

From Druid rituals to the rites of ancient Egypt, from Athens and Rome to India and Japan, morning has borne a primacy of time, a burden of hope.

I do not fear the darkness or what moves by night. In fact, I cannot tolerate much light in the room where I sleep, and sometimes I will stand at night in our yard—really no more than a brief clearing in the forest—and listen to the buzz-saw madness of cicadas in August or the crackling of hickory limbs when a winter storm nears.

But I feel nothing spiritual in the darkness, no promises, no insights. Much of this is doubtless because of history and genetics, but I think it is deeper than that. Some of the most deeply moving religious services I've ever attended have been at night, either at Christmas or in Lent, and yet there is something *planned* about such moments, almost calculated. Sure, the Bible reports a pillar of fire by night to guide the pilgrims of Israel, but when God was dueling the Pharaoh with plagues and lice, he told Moses, "Get thee unto Pharaoh in the morning ..." There is power in being strong early in the day.

What is it about morning and spirituality? Obviously, the idea of renewal is a great part of it and even of survival. One doesn't have to wait for the morning papers to read the obituaries to see if you're still alive, as the old joke goes; now you can check online. So there is an element of praise for being alive another day. And yet morning can often reinforce ongoing bad news, too. The writer of Psalm 73 puts it succinctly: "For all the day long I have been plagued, and chastened every morning."

I have been chastened many mornings myself. Still, I can walk just past dawn among the dense white oaks and hickories, stand amid dogwoods and tulip poplars, and I feel the presence of something powerful and unseen. My scientific side wants to howl with derision at such comments, invoke endorphins and circadian rhythms, to chart the natural selection of my kind. Perhaps spirituality does not exist *a priori*; I can't prove that it does. But neither do I believe that superstition and fear can account for the pervasive nature of faiths among all the peoples of the world.

Morning, to me, is spirituality's right hand, its eager accomplice in begging for belief. The writer of Psalm 90 understood this, and it's worth quoting six verses to make the point:

1. Lord, thou hast been our dwelling place in all generations.

2. Before the mountains were brought forth, or ever thou hadst formed the earth and the world, even from everlasting to everlasting, thou art God.

3. Thou turnest man to destruction; and sayest, Return, ye children of men.

4. For a thousand years in thy sight are but as yesterday when it is past and as a watch in the night.

5. Thou carriest them away as with a flood; they are as a sleep: in the morning they are like grass which groweth up.

6. In the morning, it flourisheth, and groweth up; in the evening it is cut down and withereth.

Verses 5 and 6 constitute one of the few times in the Bible that "morning" is used more than two verses in a row. (In Exodus 16, the word is used four times in the space of five verses!)

Morning has brought me plenty of remorse, some of it in my early years from over-exuberant partying or awakening to memories of serial stupidities. But there has never been a time since I was a boy that I did not feel closer to some innate sense of the spiritual when morning came. If I had been with Moses, he wouldn't have let me come up the mountain with him, but I would have been awake and watching him head off.

My heritage is Christian and includes the Bible, which I take as an inspiration from the God in us but not the "literal" word of God as fundamentalists do. But when I speak of spirituality and morning, I would not limit it to one faith. In fact, morning all but begs for pantheism if one is attuned to spirituality. Emerson, no fundamentalist himself, said the "blue zenith" of the stars and the universe "is the point in which romance and reality meet."

Religions need the morning. Of course they have lived by moon phases, flood and famine, too, all signs to be interpreted by the wise men (and women) of the tribe. That intersection of romance and reality is also the locus of spirituality. To me it is a subtle and quiet place. I have long believed that those who shout loudest about religion are not trying to convince others but themselves. Ardor is often born in fear, and, of course, so is religion. Prayer may have begun on a night of violent storms when, in the epiphanies of lightning, some man or woman saw a tiger nearby, burning bright. The spirituality of morning, more likely, began in thanksgiving. Psalm 5:3 says, "My voice shalt thou hear in the morning, O Lord; in the morning will I direct my prayer unto thee, and will look up."

Jesus in Revelation didn't say he was like the heavens at night but was "the bright and morning star." That is, something that in the dawn partakes both of night and morning.

The movie *Ladyhawke* (1985) is, as *Leonard Maltin's Movie & Video Guide* says, about "two star-crossed lovers caught in an evil spell." The film's twist on ancient love stories is that by night the man turns into a wolf and by day, his lover turns into a hawk. Thus, they can never see each other as humans and must feel yearning for something that remains another species.

The only time they may see each other as humans, and then only fleetingly, is the moment just before the sun breaks the horizon. This "so-near-yet-so-far" theme is a chestnut, but it's beautifully realized in the film, especially by Michelle Pfeiffer's incandescent performance. It seems to me that this idea is very much freighted with spiritual overtones.

That moment when light first transects the horizon with a dazzling rush can operate in the realm of the miraculous for those attuned to it. Only when the male lover, Navarre, realizes that he can dig a pit and thereby keep the sunlight off his lover long enough for him to see her as a woman, does the epiphany occur. It is a moment of deeply moving loss, for it mimics a return from the grave of a loved one, something we wish to believe can happen in real life. Since it can't, we have transposed it to a place of final rest and peace called heaven.

Though I find spirituality an easy road to travel, I find science just as interesting and often more rewarding. By relegating science to a secondary level below faith, fundamentalists lose sight of something incredibly beautiful in its own right. Morning as a spiritual metaphor has great power, but so does the unclenching of a morning glory or the erasure of the night's weight of humidity.

Still, to deny the power of morning's historical and intuitive ties to spirituality shortchanges dawn. *The Odyssey* is "morning-saturated," to use the kind of compound term that Homer (or whomever) found attractive. It invokes the gods, prays for safe guidance from night until morning, and raises omens or blessings depending on the weather and its signs.

To imagine the inhabitants of Stonehenge celebrating the morning in their sacred place (as it surely must have been) doesn't require us to stretch our imaginations much at all. We can intuit the scene, make sense of their praise, and admire their steadfastness.

Religion has been rightly blamed for many wars throughout history, even for genocide and a collapse of logical thinking. Sometimes, men have gone on crusades to whip the "infidels" into shape and make them see the "light." Early settlers in America were relentless in trying to turn hunter-gatherer societies into parishes with hymns and signs of the cross. I am willing to believe that many of these Europeans were well intentioned, and judging one era's commonplace life by another era's is folly. Still, there are times when it is clear, even from the beginning, that proselytizing is a corruption, and that instead of light, the only thing being spread is a perpetual darkness.

Just so, our spiritual attachments to morning have changed and will continue to change. Very few of us live in the country anymore but see sunrise (if ever at all) over a suburban lawn or a city street. (First light on the upper stories of skyscrapers in Manhattan is breathtaking, and even more poignant after 9/11.) But it is in the country that morning can be most spiritual because there are relatively fewer distractions.

I have seen sunrise, for example, over an interstate highway with six lanes of tractor-trailer trucks going 85 miles an hour. Nothing spiritual there except in its polar opposite. The only good thing about such a scene is there may be comparatively fewer drunks on the road at sunrise than, say at 2:00 A.M. If I invoke God at such times, it is seeking his damnation of the monstrous acts the other drivers are committing against sanity.

Give me the 7 acres of our woods on Wildcat Ridge, though, and I will spin you a morning story of the spiritual that comes from deep inside myth and religion and wonder.

Late August, almost September. A blanket of dense Gulf air has been humped over North Georgia for weeks, tropical and heavy with airborne oceans. Each morning when I step outside in the darkness, the sheer weight of the wet air oppresses me. The stars can scarcely break through this shroud of humidity. My glasses fog over instantly, and I have to remove them to walk up the slope.

This has gone on for days, but this morning, on a fine Friday, a different air mass has finally displaced the Gulf of Mexico, which has backed off perhaps 75 miles to the south. And so I walk into the woods where I will await an epiphany.

Huge granite boulders, which seem to have gnawed their way from the slope toward Wildcat Creek, lie majestically down the hill, and I walk there and sit. I call these my Philosophers' Stones, because I often retreat there to unravel the world's burdens. The few insights given me at these stones have been more than mundane, but less than profound. Moss spreads across the rocks, a softening, and a book cover. And yet their crevasses are filled with deadfall from the white oaks and hickories that tower overhead. (I always feel as if I am interrupting natural process when I pile up deadfall, but my aesthetic sense—and fear of forest fires—usually pushes me in winter to roam through our acreage picking up brittle limbs that lie in their vestigial glory all along the forest floor.)

What do I seek in this first light? I have spent much of my life trying to understand the nature of God and reconcile it with all faiths. Thank goodness for the Edward Abbeys of the world, naturalists and writers with strong passions, eager for confrontation and sure of their opinions. I have never been able to see the world so black and white, so when it comes to advocacy, I am an utter failure because of it.

Some parts of it come clearly to me. That we have wrecked and continue to wreck the environment seems inarguable. That those who wish to drill the Arctic National Wildlife Refuge are against conservation and see land as merely another commodity for exchange, are the enemy to me, if not outright evil. Those who pollute and those who allow (if not encourage) pollution are the enemy. Those who clear-cut, who ignore global warming, who fail to see that the Earth is a highly integrated organism that must be protected at all costs, are worthy of scorn (at best).

My good friend Eugene Odum spent a decade explaining all this to me. Gene was easily the most brilliant man I've ever known, and though he was not religious and rarely if ever spoke of anything like spirituality, he did believe in beauty passionately, and for him Nature, when operating without the meddlesome interference of humankind, approached something like the sublime. (He once took me to his small "farm" north of Athens for the sole purpose of explaining how small snails in his catchment basin proved the health of his tiny creek. It was morning, and I was so moved I was speechless.)

This morning, though, I sit among the stones and ask for a sign. Though I have a mystical side that bears refilling from time to time, it is small and quiet. Mostly, I exult in what nature bears before me, and I have spent most of my life not learning to feel the spirit more directly but to see more clearly.

I don't mean "see" metaphorically here but more or less literally. That is, I believe that spirituality can be gained by an increasingly intense involvement with the world, using all our senses. And for me, that engagement is most intense in morning when even miracles don't seem an absurd proposition

Miracles for me, however, aren't turning water into wine or casting out demons. They come in small statements, too.

A red-and-yellow wasp has killed an inchworm on the stones as I sit. I often see inchworms appearing to fly, hanging and writhing from a single thread from a limb, bouncing back and forth like gymnasts warming up for an exercise routine. This worm, however, is stowed along the underside of the wasp's thorax for its journey to an eating place.

The worm is motionless, clearly dead or paralyzed into a quiet coming death. The wasp tentatively tries to lift off from the stones several times, but the burden is too great for flight. Perplexed, it waddles back and forth testing its flight dynamics and finding none exist. I get down on my hands and knees and watch the struggle from 8 inches, a giant presence that the wasp seems to ignore. If she scents or senses me, she doesn't panic or even let on.

She has been successful in her hunt, though capturing an inchworm doesn't exactly seem a great challenge. But it is plump and green, filled to its epithelial cells with life, and the wasp is determined to take it away for a nice slow breakfast. I can't tell how she has secured it to her—perhaps with some of the worm's own sticky substance or something exuded from the thorax. Despite my admiration for ants, I have written about insects rarely in my career and really can't see how a green worm the size of a 1-inch section of spaghetti noodle has been stowed.

Parable intrudes here. The wasp needs the worm to live, but she's gathered a larger burden than she can carry. What's the solution? She walks splay-legged back and forth over the rocks for forty minutes, getting nowhere and sometimes stopping to see if she can lift off. But no luck. She has a great meal and can't take it away.

It's no wonder that early on we codified the wages of sin. Not that even a primitive man could see sin in this situation, but in nature, we seek analogies to human behavior, believing, against considerable evidence, that man is the measure of all things. A wasp has become "greedy" and "bitten off more than she can chew," and therefore may miss out on the meal altogether. We thus say humans are punished for overreaching, for believing they deserve more than they have rightly earned.

Society these days gives us Nietzsche in spades, but religion turns it around. A wasp may fail in her bid to take away a great feast, but, according to the fifth book of Matthew, "Blessed are they which to hunger and thirst after righteousness: for they shall be filled." So, a worm meal, no, but righteousness, yes.

Choose wisely, we might say, and that becomes a tenet of many religions.

Religions arose in part, I believe, from a close reading of nature and an attempt to understand it. What we could not understand, we ascribed to supernatural means. And because night was a time of fear and guarding, philosophy may have made its greatest strides in the morning rather than in the night, when our ancestors sat fretful in the firelight. At night one could hear nature, but only at dawn did such struggles as this wasp and worm become clear and bear the weight of metaphor and religion.

The Bible's God seemed to understand this perfectly. The first two chapters of the thirty-fourth chapter of Exodus make it explicit:

And the Lord said unto Moses, Hew thee two tables of stone like unto the first: and I will write upon these tables the words that were in the first tables which thou breakest.

And be ready in the morning, and come up in the morning unto Mount Sinai, and present thyself there to me in the top of the mount.

Moses was already a morning person, but in this command, God made implicit the idea that clarity and light are allied in many ways, and that faith believes in the new day.

Morning's Second Sense: Hearing

September is about to unwrinkle over Wildcat Ridge, borne on the sounds of dawn. This is the last weekend in August. The season's final swallowtails yesterday fluttered 30 feet into the white oak canopy, rarely lighting, sensing, perhaps, that the days of puddling and exulting are nearly gone. Chlorophyll has not yet begun to withdraw from the leaves, but a few poplar and hickory leaves have dried and washed to the ground on a mild wind.

I am lying spread eagle in the leaf litter of a dark morning, protected by insect repellant, not wishing to arise with a burden of chiggers and other insect bites. But I have put none above my shoulders so I might hear what lies beneath me without chemically urging it to flee.

I will not hear the wild diving shriek of the red-tailed hawks for several hours yet, for this is the country of owls and millipedes. Even now, a great horned owl down the creek is singing, answered by one perhaps half a mile away. If a third arose, they could be the Three Tenors, so strong is their vocalizing. In this time before morning, the forest seems to glide on sounds.

There is just enough light for me to see, but what I hear is the slight movement of something sinuous in the litter. I consider my peril for a moment, since pit vipers are attracted by heat, and every rattlesnake in Oconee County, for all I know, could be heading my way. But I've walked this land carefully for many years and seen only a few snakes, and those all beneficial, mostly black snakes and red water snakes. (I've heard since I was a boy that water moccasins live here but have never seen one. And I know what a real water moccasin looks like, since my friend, the marvelous scientist, naturalist, and writer Whit Gibbons, took me snake hunting on swampland at the Savannah River Ecology Laboratory's land near Aiken, South Carolina, a few years back. There, they put computer chips in the pits in snakes' heads to track them and examine their habitat. This "pit-tagging" is among the jobs I would like least on the planet.)

I push back the litter and see just what I expected: earthworms—perhaps ten of them, buckling against exposure and trying to reclaim invisibility. They dive into the humus with great purpose, and I close my eyes to turn their twisting into sound. An earthworm slicing into the soil has almost no sound at all, even with my ear practically on them. Darwin, late in life, became obsessed with earthworms, and for good reason. They are the earth's real gardeners, aerating acres and refreshing soil fertility with stealth and tilth.

But I'm after larger sounds of morning. I lie for as long as I dare before sitting up. And I hear it almost immediately: the slow quadrupedal crunching of a doe. A deer's steps give away its level of fear, and I can tell that I have not been seen or scented, for this deer walks with the casual clomp of someone taking what in the nineteenth century was called a "constitutional." My instinct is to look around for it, but I have come for hearing, and so, against that urge, I shut my eyes tightly.

Deer families often graze our woods. More than once, I have spoken to them in the high voice one uses with small children, and they are interested or confused enough to stand still or move away without their flight-response kicking in. Now, I say nothing. And I know it is a single deer, stepping slowly through the woods down near the creek, stopping to feed, to listen. It strikes me that if I were eating grass, we would be doing exactly the same thing.

I listen to her for perhaps ten minutes before her hoof-steps disappear into the distance. Something else now: a start-stop, start-stop, start-stop, also in the leaf litter, something very small. Against my plans, I open my eyes, and at first I see nothing, then there it is: an adult male brown thrasher—Georgia's state bird—idly hunting for bugs and worms not 30 feet from me. I try to remain motionless, but it takes only a bare movement of my head for the thrasher to sense my presence and leap upward. I close my eyes and listen for the sound of wings, but I hear nothing.

As day begins to rise, songbirds awaken to their voices, and a few crows bark, sounding like someone with a very bad hangover sitting on the edge of the bed begging for relief. *Do not move*, I tell myself. *Wait*. To know the sounds of morning, do not be part of them.

And yet I hear my own breathing now, and the wind is so calm that I take notice of my heart. I have a mechanical mitral valve in the center of my heart, a lid of carbon alloy set in a Teflon sewing ring. In quiet rooms or on silent days, I tick like a clock or a bomb, and I know that in the world of metaphor and medicine, I partake of both.

On a morning two years ago, I heard death in this very place, too. I was doing much the same thing—standing as quietly as possible and inhaling the morning with my senses, knowing too well that I missed most of it. Then: a humping thrash and a pause, a humping thrash and a pause.

There, off to my left: a dying hawk. I was stunned to see this majestic bird moving on its wings like an old man with crutches. Perhaps age or mischance or even West Nile Virus. I did not move. Its hop and scratch were deeply moving to me and yet I did not want to interfere with its passing, for such a keen raptor, once king of the fields, deserves a dignified death.

Its wings, once red-brown and strong enough to keep it aloft for long hunting flights, were extended and useless. It crept along painfully until finally, turning, it saw me and froze.

It's something of a commonplace that we have lost touch with our hunting origins. Well-meaning men and women still persist in loading on to Native Americans all the trappings of a Rousseauian noble savage, complete with perpetual high-mindedness and a close, nourishing relationship with the Earth. I have read extensively in American Indian history, both of my own land and the Great Plains, and even considering the blather of New Age sages, there is something profoundly touching and genuine about how most Indians viewed the Earth. We have come so far from those ideas that our current administration as I write this seems more intent on unilaterally destroying the Earth than saving it.

I have known hunters all my life who are decent, educated men and women, who understand the balance of nature and see good coming from a successful deer hunt. But they are the exception, for most hunters I have known would shoot (and often have) anything that moves on the off chance that its head might be worth mounting in the den. I am not sure if animals have "rights," but no living creature deserves such disrespect.

They may be no finer hunter than the red-tailed hawk, able to spot a mouse from a hundred feet and to dive down with killing precision to the spot where the running rodent will be seven seconds later. Western tradition doesn't especially ask me to back off and let this creature have a dignified death, but American Indian ways do. (I may be one of the few Americans who will say, flat out, that there is absolutely no evidence of Indian blood in my family. My wife's father's family has the tradition of a Blackfoot ancestor, so I can at least say it's possible my children have that heritage, but I don't.)

So I averted my eyes, turned as quietly as I could, and walked away. A week later, my beagle Murphy walked slowly up to the front porch with a hawk foot, claws and all, in her mouth, and I gently took it away and buried it in the woods. Perhaps the spirit of hawks makes a morning noise, too.

Something smaller but insistent: crickets. There's a lot to admire in crickets, not the least of which is their lively and chipping morning song. Unlike cicadas, whose buzz in the forest in late summer is enough to make humans (and not just beagles) howl, crickets spread balm.

Of course, to pest control companies, crickets are the enemy, and there's a huge business for owners of perfect suburban lawns who want to kill their burden of mole crickets. Since we live in the country and the woods, our crickets are welcome to munch on whatever they wish. The idea of trying to wipe them out would be laughable, even if I wanted to, and I don't.

Orthoptera, from the Greek *ortho* meaning straight and *ptera* meaning wing, refers to the parallel-sided structure of the front wings or tegmina of grasshoppers, locusts, katydids, and crickets. These plant-feeding insects have been around since the Carboniferous period, which means they may well outlive humans when the final meltdown comes in a couple of billion years, give or take a million.

There are more than a thousand species of Orthoptera in the United States alone, and some 20,000 worldwide.

By singling out snooty, perfect-lawn suburbanites, I don't mean to demean the damage that Orthoptera do. In North America, Asia, and Africa, they cause billions of dollars in crop losses each year and lead to great human misery and hunger. When God was trying to nettle Pharaoh, he even sent a "plague of locusts" to torment the Egyptians. Which was probably terrible, though not as bad as turning their water into blood.

And I've been in many bait shops where the predominant sound is the Handelian chorus of crickets, cage-bound and awaiting work as fish bait. (Handel, in fact, wrote an oratorio called *Israel In Egypt*, in which he composed music about the legendary plagues visited by a wrathful God, and it includes, among other things, an odd hop-skipping bit of music set to the words "their land brought forth frogs.")

The crickets that own Wildcat Ridge are neither pests nor bait. They will never have a postage stamp in their honor, though the government of Malawi printed a stamp with a red locust, perhaps in honor of its power and as a way to ask it to stay the hell away.

Male crickets chirp to attract mates. They do this by something called stridulation—rubbing the upper surface of one wing against the lower surface of another wing, or the inner surface of the hind leg against the outer surface of the front wing. The mating call of every "stridulating species" is unique, and sometimes their morphology is so similar that the mating call is the only way to distinguish them.

Crickets that produce these sounds also have "ears"—on their front legs. (Stridulating grasshoppers have "ears" on their first abdominal segment.) Some species can makes sounds at a mind-boggling 100 kilohertz, though humans wouldn't know it, since the higher range of our hearing ability is about 20 kHz.

Which means that what we hear of this morning cricket chorus is a fraction of what's actually out there. (Lest we feel superior, one species, the snowy tree cricket, actually recites the *temperature*. Add forty to the number of chirps it makes in fifteen seconds, and you'll have the temperature in Fahrenheit. Science is full of fascinating and moderately useless bits of such information.)

I spend about ten minutes listening to the crickets sing before I hear something else: *keeer, keeer, keeer.*

~

I once told my father that the red-tailed hawk was my favorite bird. He, a child of the Depression when a chicken lost to a hawk might have meant a missed meal, looked at me with mild horror. With dozens of species of beautiful and tuneful birds, why on earth would I pick a raptor whose song is a wild shriek?

I think part of it is the hawk's sheer arrogance. Hawks love to make keen-eyed turns looking for unwitting birds and small mammals. We have those, but we also have a red-tail who sits on the power lines near our recycling center, big as a small penguin, awaiting vermin to come sort the trash. This may seem an ignoble way to make a living, but I rather admire the guy, and when he stares at the traffic, he does it with such disdainful panache you have to admire his vocation.

I close my eyes and let the red-tails have my aural attention. I have read numerous descriptions of their screech from nature writers and scientists over the years, but it still sounds like *keeer, keeer, keeer* to me. Our woods are the homeland of hawks, and though I've seen red-shouldered hawks and kestrels, their smaller cousins, our predominant species by far is the arrogant red-tail.

He thinks—no, he *knows*—you are his inferior. I've stood at a good angle from a tall branch many times and watched a red-tail watching me, eyes eagle-browed, gaze intense and unforgiving, superior status assured. In fact, I could swear I've seen red-tails *sneer*, which would suit their personalities.

Year round, we hear the morning screech of red-tailed hawks, and that wild song never fails to bless me. This morning, though, a cloud cover rolls in, and the red-tails suddenly go quiet. Perhaps, robbed of depth perception, they go roost and wait. If you're a free-living hawk, not bound by dumpster or the pigeons of a high-rise, you can wait.

Then human sounds wake me, as T. S. Eliot would have it, and I drown. A few badly mufflered cars growl past, out on Oliver Bridge Road, rednecking along with bad springs and tubercular engines. A jet, having taken off fifteen minutes before from Atlanta, defaces the sky. Kid noises through the woods from the house to our west.

And I realize yet again that there is no such thing as a morning sound; just *morning sounds wherever you are.* Some are the same; many are different. None of this gives me comfort.

The crickets have gone silent. Someone drives down the dirt road on which we live, crackling gravel and spinning dust. I try very hard to believe that morning and its sounds are not ruined entirely. But it's no use, so I go back inside to my desk and put on a CD of symphonies by Marcel Landowski and listen to my fingers pounding this computer keyboard. I look out the window over the woods toward Wildcat Creek, and not even a whiff of breeze rattles the leaves. Megan is downstairs watching cartoons. Linda is making coffee and listening to the news on NPR.

The air conditioner breathes comfort and consumption. Two of my cats are dashing madly all over the house, as if one were predator and one were prey.

Oh What a Beautiful Morning: Impression–Sunrise

My first published novel, *The Heart of a Distant Forest* (W. W. Norton and Co., 1984), begins this way:

> *Morning is rising in silence. Nothing will happen along the green edge of the pond for several minutes more. I rest among a tangle of ferns. At the far edge of the water's mirror are* Typha latifolia, *common cattails, erect and masculine, stalk-straight as the light edges from the east.*

That image of morning and silence has been one I have cherished all my life. I was so nervous when the book's first printing was due that I originally missed a ghastly typo: In the hardback it says "at the far edge of the water's *edge*" instead of *mirror*. I didn't even see the error until I was reading aloud in the University of Georgia Art Museum and came to that word, stumbled, and looked, I'm sure, like an idiot. (The mistake was corrected in later editions.)

I suppose more books, paintings, and music have been about night than morning. I still remember the first recording I heard, in the late 1950s, of Schubert's stunning song *Das Erlkönig*, and its hoof beats of Death coming after a rider in the darkness. I all but wore the grooves off the

LP of the song, as sung by Elly Ameling, in my teenage years.

Even then, however, night was something of a mystery to me. In truth, I have stayed awake all night only once in my life, at an all-night horror-movie festival in college when I was a senior, and I only did that to impress my girlfriend (and future wife) Linda. She wasn't all that impressed, but it took me three days to recover.

I do know something of the night. A few days ago, I went to my brother Mark's house a mile or so from mine on Wildcat Ridge. True to his need to master everything, he built a 10-inch reflecting telescope, then designed and built an observatory, complete with retractable roof, to scan the stars. On this night, we were to watch Mars pass closer to Earth than it has in 60,000 years, but a glitch in one axis motor limited us to a brief, low-resolution glimpse of the Bringer of War.

The night, however, was splendid, with the Milky Way brushed overhead like glitter in a wash of watercolor. Mark's wife Anne brought me back to reality, though, as we stood in the pasture.

"Watch out for the fire ant nests," she said. "They're all over the place."

An entire art movement was kicked off by morning. Claude Monet's painting *Impression: Sunrise* was derided when it was first hung, but its rendering of nature through feeling and suggestion rather than classical line and image, began the movement known as Impressionism—one of the nineteenth century's greatest gifts to the eye.

The painting is the size of the pre-stretched canvases you might buy at a chain discount store: 19" by 24 3/8". But its impact on the world of art was enormous.

John Rewald, in his *History of Impression*, captures the moment:

"Monet later explained that he had selected for the exhibition a painting done in Le Havre from his window: the sun appearing in damp vapors, in the foreground a few shipmasts pointing. 'I was asked to give a title for the catalogue; I couldn't very well call it a *View of Le Havre*.' So I said: 'Put *Impression*.' Indeed, the painting was catalogued as *Impression: Sunrise*."

The power of those words has not diminished more than a century later. A play called *Impression Sunrise* premiered in 2001, for example. The travel editor for *Lonely Planet*, Don George, also in 2001 called one of his columns "Impression: Sunrise at Uluru." And if you really wanted to be intimate with Monet's sunrise, you could have, a few years ago, bought the 44"-by-66" museum-sized canvas rendering from Barnes & Noble for a mere $595.

One of the first pieces I ever learned to play on the piano was "Morning" from the *Peer Gynt Suite* by the Norwegian composer Edvard Grieg. Its gentle evocation of day coming awake, as I said earlier, is familiar enough to have been used in Warner Brothers cartoons, and its iconic status may now be more as a joke than as a work of art.

Even when morning isn't the putative subject of art, we can feel it clearly enough. I have never heard morning more aptly mimicked than in the opening movement of Gustav Mahler's *Symphony No. One*, which is subtitled "The Titan."

The movies love the image, too, even though morning, as usual, gets short shrift. There's *Sunrise at Campobello*, in which Ralph Bellamy re-played his Tony Award-winning stage performance as Franklin Roosevelt. Then there's F.W. Murnau's wonderful silent film *Sunrise* about a farmer plotting to kill his wife. There are two versions of the war movie *Dawn Patrol*, though the 1938 movie with Errol Flynn, David Niven, and the always-marvelous Basil Rathbone is by far the best. George Romero's *Dawn of the Dead* is, believe it or not, an excellent horror movie. Then there's Katherine Hepburn's superb 1933 film *Morning Glory* and Jane Fonda's moderately lousy 1986 one, *The Morning After*.

But of course, "morning" and "dawn" are metaphors here, not descriptions of the time of day. But that's how morning works in art most of the time—metaphorically. On the flip side, the films at the other end of day seem endless—*Sunset*, *Sunset Boulevard*, *Sunset Cove*, *Sunset Park*, *Sunshine*, *The Sunshine Boys*, *The Sun Shines Bright*.

And *night* rules in the movies. There are more than 130 films with "night" in the title, from *Night After Night* to *Night Zoo*.

Part of all this is the fact that what people typically do in the morning is far different from what they do at night. There are mornings of great passion, strawberries and champagne for breakfast, listening to birds welcome the day. But most of us love, laugh, relax, drink, dance, and shout in the night. Raise your hand if you've received an invitation to a party set for 6:00 A.M. I didn't think so.

So if art reflects who we are and what we do, then morning might properly reflect the physical world. People do love images of sunrise but mostly in photographs or paintings. It may well be that more people have seen

Impression: Sunrise than have seen a real sunrise, a strange and sobering thought. Tens of thousands of sunrise photographs and paintings fill the Internet, and at least one morning-hater in your office likely has a sunrise image for her computer's wallpaper.

Sunrise is dramatic, let's face it. Our limbic brains go off guard-duty against the wolves, which haven't bothered us for several hundred years. But again, it's a matter of context, in art and life. Sunrise on vacation at Edisto Island is a glory if you didn't have seven beers the night before. Dawn on your worst day of the workweek is something you want to hit with a 2-by-4.

Artists always look for moments of drama to make their points. (Well, maybe Samuel Beckett often didn't, but his eyes looked inward on genius and the dark side of a new art.) There isn't any drama at two in the afternoon except the work of trying to stay awake after lunch. Monet's *Sunrise* wasn't really about morning but about breaking up the elements of art to create an impression rather than a rendering.

One might think this was the beginning of a separation between art and science, but in my mind it wasn't so much a paradigm shift as a reflection of society. If Jackson Pollock had lived at the time of Monet, he would have been chained to a wall after exhibiting *Number One*. If Monet had lived at the time of Michelangelo, children in the street of Florence would have followed him around throwing rocks at him and making up snide rhymes. The Holy Inquisition would have burned Salvador Dalí at the stake.

Claude Debussy managed to take the whole day for himself. In his great orchestral masterpiece *La Mer*, the first movement is called "From dawn to midday on the sea." He also composed *Prelude to the Afternoon of a Faun* and beautiful *Nocturnes*. Maybe he was just hedging his bets with morning and night people. (But this also begs another question: Is there such a thing as an *afternoon person*? I can't even begin to imagine it.)

Richard Wagner wrote an entire orchestral interlude about "Dawn" into *Götterdämmerung* (*The Twilight of the Gods*). And indeed Wagner loved to write about the morning, even though he was usually up to his silk pajamas in intrigues every night of his life, being chased by creditors and jealous husbands.

As I've said before, the Romantic writers and composers often used dawn as the time when the Truth is Revealed. For decades, morning, then, wasn't a time you wanted to approach because your tryst might have been uncovered or your lover dead of dramatically quaffed poison. There's not much use for art when you're trying to figure out a way to save your ass.

———

The metaphorical importance of night and morning, however, changed with one invention: electric light. In the days of candles and oil lamps, many of things could be happening in corners, from trysts to murders. The imagination had a bit more room to maneuver. But when bright lights suddenly filled parlors and illuminated streets, there was less to imagine.

Maybe it's a coincidence that by the time electric lighting became ubiquitous, Romanticism breathed its last gasp. Most cultural historians blame World War I for the rise of a harder art, one that didn't see much joy in morning, noon, *or* night. And there's considerable evidence that they are right.

Still, as Roger Shattuck's marvelous book *The Banquet Years* points out, Romanticism had begun to fade long before the end of the nineteenth century. And in all the arts, morning had one serious and enduring enemy: alcohol. From the early 1800s on, artists (and I use the term inclusively here) were almost *expected* to be dissolute. The public, in fact, all but demanded it.

(As a side note, I was at a college writer's conference once when a very well-known Southern writer, in the early afternoon, told me: "I'll be back later, but now I have to go get drunk for the faculty." I knew exactly why he was doing it. He was as good as his word and arrived back, roaring, several hours later.)

Coleridge didn't write "Kubla Khan" in the ecstasy of dawn but reportedly late at night after awakening from an opium-influenced dream—the perfect Romantic moment (and almost the perfect Romantic poem). As the century progressed, more and more artists palliated their emotional states with drink and drugs. Writer and doctor Kay Jamison has made a fine career out of linking creativity to serious mental and emotional problems, and her work is deeply convincing, profoundly moving (Read *Touched by Fire* for instance.).

These episodes of carousing and drinking often lasted until morning, but with a few exceptions of three-day parties, dawn largely revealed the disaster of mixing highly strung creative people with absinthe and gin. I can barely imagine anything more ugly than Scott and Zelda in a screaming argument, blind-drunk, as the sun came up.

Still, even the Lost Generation appreciated the dawn. Hemingway's first full-length novel, and one many critics still believe is his best, was *The Sun Also Rises*, the title coming from Ecclesiastes, that Biblical gold mine of literary titles. Yet *The Sun Also Rises* is anything but a morning book—in fact I find it hard to believe that most of the characters, especially Lady Brett, didn't require long-term hospitalization and drying out after the fiesta of Pamplona. Hemingway said that the book was "a damn tragedy" with the Earth abiding as the hero. While critics may argue over the book's meaning and importance, there's no argument that the whole fictional crowd probably wanted to be shot when dawn came.

The Marx Brothers spent *A Night at the Opera*. Mussorgsky's *Night on Bald Mountain*, with its cinematic storm, has been used for movies and cartoons for eighty years. Cole Porter's song *Night and Day* is clearly more about a lover's dreams of night. Though Van Gogh could paint gorgeous rich canvases of daylight scenes, perhaps his most famous image is *Starry Night*—a painting I have stood and admired in the Museum of Modern Art in New York City several times.

Morning isn't exactly the Rodney Dangerfield of art because it does get some respect, metaphorically, if not often literally. Still, its dramas are subtle, and subtlety doesn't sell books or get moviegoers in the seats. When the great mansion Manderly burns at the end of Alfred Hitchcock's film *Rebecca*, it happens, of course, in the pitch black.

In more than twenty years as a published writer of books, as much has been made in the press (and personally) about my early rising to write as my books themselves. One of the first questions I get when I travel to speak or participate in writers' conferences is very familiar: "Do you still get up at four or five o'clock in the morning to write?"

One woman recently told me she wanted to write in the morning as I do, but that it took her two hours to awaken. She gave a convincing description of finally gaining consciousness around ten, two hours into the workday. I awaken immediately and am ready to write within ten minutes of opening my eyes.

This, as I have written earlier, may be less a virtue than a matter of genetics. My guess is that all my ancestors were given the morning shift to watch out for wolves and Vandals. Still, my sister Laura Jane is decidedly not a morning person, and so I can only guess how in the genetic scrambling of traits I wound up with this particular body clock.

I love to write, and so I can't wait to get back to my computer each morning. I also have no "start-up" time, since I do what Hemingway suggested in *A Moveable Feast*: Always quit for the day when you know what is going to happen next. That way, you can jump right back in. I am also nearly comatose by ten in the evening, and together these may explain why I have treated morning in my books with more affection than most writers do.

For every "Chelsea Morning," we have a dozen *All-Night Vigil*s. (The former song was written and sung by Joni Mitchell and the latter, also sometimes called *Vespers*, is by Sergei Rachmaninoff.) For every *Dawn Patrol*, we have hundreds of *Night*(s) *of the Living Dead*.

And yet morning has had a profound impact on the arts, even if it sometimes occurs by default.

This may seem facile. Every day has a morning and a noon and a night, and each affects people in different ways. Artists, for the most part, however, have been out of love with morning for two centuries. In his 2003 book *A Tragic Honesty: The Life and Work of Richard Yates*, writer Blake Bailey paints a ghastly picture of mornings for the once-famous writer, who was also an alcoholic and die-hard cigarette addict. (That he had tuberculosis, that most Mimi-like disease of nineteenth-century artists, didn't help.)

Yates was given to massive benders and defiantly smoked four packs of cigarettes a day until they killed him at the startlingly late age of sixty-six. (One can only admire the human machine that can take such abuse for decades and keep working.) Most mornings for Yates consisted of sitting, whey-faced, on the side of the bed and coughing uncontrollably for half an hour or more until, wheezing and holding on to walls, he made it to the bathroom or the kitchen for coffee.

The very idea of writing early in the morning would probably have driven Yates into a foaming fit of loathing and vituperation.

But even the most jaded night person sometimes had an epiphany in the morning.

Early morning, July 1961. The morning sun must have been streaming through the windows in Ernest Hemingway's house in Ketchum, Idaho. He had been extremely ill for months with numerous physical maladies from a life of heavy drinking and exposing his body to injury. Only seven years before, he had endured two plane crashes *on consecutive days* in Africa, leaving him with massive internal injuries from which he never really healed.

He loved the morning and was often up early, though he typically didn't write before dawn. This day, however, having recently endured electroshock therapy and heavy medications, he knew that it was over.

Not in the afternoon, not at dusk, not at night, *but in the morning.* He quietly went into the basement and got his favorite shotgun and came back to the foyer of his house—a place of entrance, of arrivals and departures. There, in morning's light of knowing, he put the gun to his head and pulled the trigger.

The morning birds outside may have lifted off in surprise at the noise, wings aimed toward the rising sun.

River Morning

We come from beneath the dripping shade of a green canopy to the edge of the river. The sharp light of a July morning skitters across the strong current of the Oconee as it moves south, cutting through farmland and forest. My brother Mark and I get ready to slide the fiberglass canoe into the ancient riverbed.

This isn't *Deliverance*. The Oconee River this summer is half dry due to drought, and normally it is a flat placid canoe trip from this point only half a mile east of Wildcat Ridge to our take-out point at a ranger station where the Highway 15 bridge crosses into Greene County.

A few days earlier, I'd dropped by Hot Thomas's barbecue place out on the highway and told him that Mark and I were going to canoe the Oconee on Friday morning. He grinned, a quiet and pleasant man.

"Is there enough water in it for that?" he asked as he bagged dinner for my family.

"Just barely," I said. "I've heard old people have never seen it this low."

"I heard you can walk across it any place you want to," he said. "You all don't drown."

I'm not thinking of drowning this morning, though, but of distant imperatives, mythic stories of brothers and waters, of great mounds of earth, of chiefdoms and land. All week I have dreamed myself into the moment: gliding down the river beneath the overhung canopy of beech and elm and a thousand shrubs with a thousand names.

We're putting in on the land of some people Mark knows. We've already parked my car at the Highway 15 bridge, driven the 8 miles back north in his old truck, and now pull the canoe out into the wet morning grass. I'm careful with my back, which is crackered with degenerating disks, but I'm determined. Shafts of sunlight drive themselves through the canopy of trees and into the eddies and swift-running current.

Mark is only eighteen months older than I am, and we grew up in the woods and fields of north central Georgia, camping for days in the sweet stifling air of summer. Now, he is an archaeologist at the University of Georgia where I am a science writer and sometime teacher of creative writing, and we are headed down the river, true, but we are also headed for holy ground.

"Hold it there," he says as we ease the green canoe into the water. "I'll get the gear in." He loads paddles, water, a few snacks. "Okay." He has already driven the truck back a couple of dozen yards from the river into a safer place, and we are ready to shove off.

I am exultant, proud that in my age, with a chest torn open a few years before to receive an artificial mitral valve, I can head into the river with Mark. No human structures will be visible from the river. This land is still too far from the conveniences most people find necessary for life—malls, grocery stores, and fast food. It is still in some ways a wild place, green and gray, filled with birdsong and the wild angles of diving raptors.

"I'm getting in the bow," I say, and I climb into the canoe as Mark holds it from the bank. We have debated the craft's orientation before we climb in, and we decide to let it hang straight downstream, south with the current.

"Okay, hold it steady," Mark says, and he's climbing in. But before he is seated, our balance has suddenly gone terribly wrong, and I'm holding on with both hands, rocking madly. In trying to keep from falling, I choose the one move that guarantees we cannot hold the current, and with a shocking suddenness, I am pitched to starboard and into the river.

While the river itself is shallow with drought, we have chosen to enter it at one place where it is deep from centuries of undercutting the soft bottom of the riverbank. I spent much of one summer studying the dunes beneath Wildcat Creek, and I know that stream and river bottoms can change radically in flood or even drought.

My jeans are heavy, and I turn once and see Mark fall into the river before I am drawn downward over my head into a riverbank hole. I know immediately that this drought-starved river, of which we had made fun, is trying to kill me. I am churned downward and then farther again, and I'm thrashing in utter darkness, for the morning light has no home here. My sneakers catch on root-matter. The water turns me once, then, twice, and I grope for anything within reach and feel only primal water. I flail as if I had wings.

Suddenly, as if ejecta from a volcanic fissure, I am rising, rising, and I break the surface of the water with my eyes. I gasp, being thrown against the riverbank, washed rapidly downstream. I cannot find the river bottom nor can I reach the gnarled tree roots, which grip the bank like the talons of an old man. I turn ahead and see, 20 feet downstream, a clot of distended limbs and roots, and when I am pushed into them, I hold on, saved. I am spitting water and have already decided—in the few moments the entire episode took—that I will act as if nothing has happened but a stupid accident.

The river tries to pulls me off my limb-roost, but it doesn't make much effort. The water here is still well over my head. I yell at Mark that I'm all right, and he's already scrambling out of the river, having somehow managed to hold on to the canoe. Some of our gear comes floating straight toward me, and I grab it and hang on. I turn and look at the riverbank about 10 feet away, and it rises straight up, with no handholds or easy escapes. Not there.

"I've got to float down a bit to get out," I say. A crow not far away is sitting on a limb watching me with stupefied curiosity. Mark says something about being careful, but I cannot stop thinking of the current at the bottom of that hole, its feral grasp on me. I have in my life known people who have died by drowning, known them personally, and that imagined frustration and terror before a final acceptance makes me tremble.

Hemingway, as a young man, wrote that "the world breaks us all, and afterward, many are strong at the broken places," but the only thing that occurs to me is that I am soaked and shivering and that I will *die* before I cancel our trip. I can't stay in this root-knot, and I can't climb out here, so I secure the few supplies I've snagged and put out into the current and orient myself in the morning light to live as a water creature.

"Careful!" Mark shouts. But by now I have found my water shape, and I can steer in the river as if born to it. Another 20 feet, there are more roots, and I latch on and pause. The bank is now even steeper and more densely wooded, and so, after I catch my breath, I push outward yet again.

This time, I feel an almost idiotic peace, as if my body has been redesigned for drifting, and I watch the bank stream past me, bearing sunstruck lizards on rotten logs, sunny patches of roots dipped into the water like mangroves, sipping life through their root-straws. Twenty, thirty yards. I am drenched and exultant when I reach a flat cove where glistening brown sand fans into the water of the Oconee. I come to it and swing my legs up and out and sit, heaving for breath.

I sit for about two minutes after shouting back that I'm fine. Then I climb up the bank, pulling myself from root to trunk, and come to a flat path trod down by deer and boys, and in less than five minutes, I've slogged, waterlogged, back to where we put into the water. I'm grinning slightly.

"Well, you screwed up," I say.

"*Me*?" he says. "That was all your fault." We've been doing this for half a century, and its ritual aspects are comforting. "Do you want to go on and do this?"

"Hell, yes," I say.

I was once to share a billing with M. Scott Momaday at a writers' conference in Colorado, but at the last moment, he had to cancel, and I was deeply sorry. His books, specifically speaking of his Kiowa heritage, have changed me, and I wanted to tell him that. In *The Way to Rainy Mountain*, he wrote, "The Kiowas are a summer people; they abide the cold and keep to themselves, but when the season turns and the land becomes warm and vital they cannot hold still; an old love of going returns upon them."

I have never had that old love of going, though I have seen some of my own country. But this morning, I want to go down this river worse than anything I have done in many years, and the malevolent intent of a current-strong pool will not stop me. (Fortunately for me, the great William Kittredge was at the same conference, and I did get to read with him.)

And so we start all over again, securing things, gaining a better balance, soaked and laughing, and in a single push we drive with our paddles into the heart of the river and push south.

Once in mid-water, flowing smoothly before the blades of our paddles, we can see just how shallow the river is: not more than 3 feet in the middle, less in other places. I start laughing, thinking only a fool could drown in such a shrunken piece of river. Still, it is probably 60 yards wide, and there is, thankfully, little sign of human life along its banks. Mark and I tickle the river's back with our paddles and push easily into the stream.

Paddling a drought-starved river in the morning is a strange experience. I can lean over slightly to my side and see the river bottom flowing beneath me, 3 feet down, and there is a feeling that we're in a theme park, ready to be stopped and taken off the ride by a tattooed teenager wearing khaki and a bored frown. Sometimes, through the flora on the Oconee's banks, we can see small herds of beef cattle that have come to water and look up at us as if seeing some rare, strange creatures.

Domesticated animals are rare, though, and for forty minutes into our 8-mile-trip, we glide along beneath the arch of great blue herons.

"I'd like to see an eagle here," I say from my front seat.

"Might," Mark says. "Up from the lake."

The lake, 20 miles to the south, is Lake Oconee, yet another hydroelectric blot on the landscape, and a dark herald of the Anti-Wilderness. It has brought millionaires, posh hotels, and marinas. In general, I despise such destruction of lovely river valleys, but like all humans I'm inconsistent in my disgusts. Mark and I own a pontoon boat, in fact, which we keep at Blue Springs Marina and take out on the lake when the weather is nice. Still, when I glide over the site of the ferry that took travelers across the river at Park's Mill, I feel sick to my soul at what has been destroyed.

Lake Oconee has changed the fauna of the area, too, and now ospreys build huge nests in the crooks of exposed trees in the water, lodgings that look like an overstuffed chair that has exploded, blowing timber in all directions. It has also brought a few bald eagles, something I thought I could never see in my homeland. (As a boy, seeing a deer in these parts was like seeing a vision in a Wagner opera, so rare were whitetails. Now, the descendants of animals brought in by hunters to kill for "sport" are wreaking their revenge by showing up by the dozens in the middle of our towns, eating away beds of hostas and other tender, tasty plants. I say more power to them. I hope when Georgia is finally eaten to the ground, the last herd turns out the lights when they leave and opens the floodgates of the dams since we won't need electricity anymore.)

Here, though, we are far from the roar of outboard engines, the jostle of humanity. And, to be fair, a lake can also be a poor man's pleasure, and fishing—which I did with a vengeance for more than twenty years on the lake—can put supper on the table. Still, all my life I have sought a more perfect solitude, one that drives me like an arrow into the heart of the natural world. I once exulted through a morning in a pass some 12,000 feet high just outside Aspen, far above the tree line, where snow held in

July, but this is my home country, green and wet, heavy with heat in summer, glorious in autumn, choked with the fecund float of pollen from a thousand different plants in spring.

Mark and I aren't sentimental companions. We've argued cheerfully and often since childhood, but we've never had a serious argument since we became teenagers, and now, stroking the river together, we are moving the canoe through the clear green-brown water, perfectly balanced.

After a long while, we see a large sandbar on the river's eastern bank.

"Let's pull in for a while," Mark says, and without speaking I agree, shifting my paddle to starboard to dig hard through the current. I'm out first, standing in ankle deep water, and I drag the canoe up on to the sand, where it seats itself firmly. I can see right away that we aren't going to be able to play Lewis and Clark here in this fragrant morning. The bank has been beaten down by the saucer-sized hoof prints of cattle, which have clearly been coming here for many years to water. Through the limbs of a lace-bark elm, I can see on an upslope a hundred yards away, some Angus-Hereford crosses that are lazily cropping the stunted grass in a pasture. Farmers don't have to fence off a river because cows will avoid a bank if they can't see the bottom or the other side.

"Damn, look at this place," I say with admiration. Even with the hoof prints of cattle in evidence, this bend in the Oconee River is a land of green luxury, overhung by beech and elm and hickory trees. Deadfall floats past in the river, turning in an elegant ballet that would seem fine if set to something by Tchaikovsky.

"I told you," says Mark, who's paddled this stretch before. I have almost forgotten about our earlier spill.

"And the light, my God," I say. The morning here, without a man-made sound in evidence, seems home to all the songbirds of north central Georgia, and in their dozens they sing and flutter through the canopy and above it. But what leaves me nearly breathless is the softness, the genuine benevolence, of the light.

A solitary morning on a river takes one to the very edge of heaven. Once when I was camping on the Tallulah River in far northeast Georgia, I rose just at dawn and hop-stepped over the dry rocks to the center of the flow and sat. Dawn sifted through the trees like floating flour. I put on my earphones and fiddled with the dial until South Carolina Public Radio came drifting to me, and I sat in mid-river listening to Beethoven. The moment was transcendent, since Beethoven loved nature, too, and created many of his best works while on solitary tramps in the woods around Vienna.

Perhaps a more perfect solitude would not involve manmade sounds, but I'd feel sorry for the person who could not exult in Beethoven while sitting at dawn in the middle of a river.

I kneel on the sandbar and look at the congress of mica flecks that meets and argues with the sunlight. I see drifted and water-smooth pine-knots spun out in their lovely grotesqueries. To my left is a small potsherd from a vessel made 500 years before. I pick it up and look for decorations, but there are none. We chase the ceremonial in our ancestry, but they lived plebian daily lives, too.

Mark and I once tramped the woods as boys, but now we are graying and past fifty. And yet the old feelings return, the ability to pretend this is adventure, that disaster might reach us around the next bend, that we might find ourselves in a ghost town, hearing the voices of a century past.

After a pleasant break, we carefully get back into the canoe and push into the current, now a perfectly balanced team, digging the foam with purposeful strokes. For a long time we pass down the shallow river, and I keep an eye out for any signs of benthic life, from crawfish to bass, but all I see are gorgeous clots of light-shot vegetation, waving us onward.

There are no signs of humans, nothing. Not a trotline or a fishing path to the water's edge. More than once, it appears we will have to portage since in places the water is less than 2 feet deep. And yet the canoe ignores the river's embarrassment and glides in a lordly stride over its back southward. Sunny shoals lift their shoulders out of the riverbed, shrugging as we pass. The riverbed sometimes falls away and the water nears 5 or 6 feet, but in most places, if we spill, we would be, at worst, in smoothly flowing, waist-deep water. As I said, this isn't *Deliverance*.

"It's just ahead," Mark says after we've paddled through the near-wilderness for another twenty minutes. And with those words, I feel a strong sense of history and wonder, for we are heading to the Scull Shoals mound site, where Indians lived several hundred years ago. I've been here once or twice before, but never from the river. Mark spent two summers here, in 1983 and 1985, directing summer archaeological field schools that mapped the sites and did some excavations.

We turn the canoe and beach it, then walk through a dense wood for a hundred yards.

"Where the hell are we?" I ask. Insects are all but smacking their lips at the prospect of this twin source of blood meals.

"Just hold on," he says, looking around. "I know we're just about in the right place."

We walk a hundred yards north, find nothing, then turn east again and come back around in an arc. I'm starting to doubt him when we see, through the silent stand of hardwoods, an impressive and somehow disturbing sight: a mound of earth that seems like something volcanic, as if it had erupted from the floodplain.

"Look at *that*," I say. And we are suddenly using trees to pull ourselves to the top of this mound, which has survived the ravages of pothunters for many years. These cultural thieves, through ignorance or malice, destroy historic sites, and some of the holes in the mound have the feel of tragedy. Still, the shape and integrity of the mound is intact, and the knowledge generated by Mark and other archaeologists who have worked at the site, is impressive. There is, in fact, another, smaller mound, nearby, but from the top of the main mound, you can see the flat land and its tangle of trees and undergrowth in all directions.

Even though it's nearly midmorning, the light is thin in here—and we do have the distinct sense of being inside something. The mounds are covered with trees, some of them thick trunked and venerable. I can imagine this land cleared, and dozens of Indians cooking and visiting, speaking of rumors, wars, rivers, sunlight, morning. I am careful to step lightly, for in a real sense, this is holy ground.

We have become accustomed through culture to tread lightly on another's man's religion, to avoid the appearance of disrespect or blasphemy. The casual anti-Semitism and racism that popped up like an evil spirit in early twentieth century correspondence and speech has mostly faded. I am old enough to remember water fountains in my hometown's courthouse labeled "white" and "colored." And yet we somehow have not yet extended the equal courtesy of abandoning racism to Native Americans. Until we accept that past reality as equally valid, we will never understand who we are or what we have done.

The sifting light, the quiet breeze that has risen, the sound of my brother's footsteps—all these instill me with a respect for *place* and the people who were here first. We linger for a while, but the river is still moving back there, and the current that bore us this far has made its way miles south by now. Besides, there is another ghost town in this place, and we have planned to stop there and walk around and inhale the morning there as well.

Oddly, it isn't as easy to find our way back to the river. You'd think one would just walk west. But we've woven our way through the woods to get to the mounds, like a shuttle in a loom, and besides, the undergrowth is too thick in places to move against. I say *against* rather than *through* deliberately, because, often, brambles can roll for hundreds of yards, and some routes are quite literally impenetrable.

"We're lost," I say after we've walked several hundred yards.

"No, we're not," says Mark, and I trust him. Of course, he's right. We come out a not far from the canoe, but he senses we're too far south, and we walk north along the river and see the canoe napping on the sandbank.

The morning buoys us along on the river, and I love the swift glide upon the water after our hike in the snaky floodplain, where we must have looked like players in a Kabuki drama as we stopped to swat mosquitoes and gnats. Here, small, self-contained swarms of insects huddle in communities just above the river to connive. Shafts of light strike through them.

I also note a pleasant sight: Trees whose roots have been undermined have collapsed into the river. And yet they have adapted and even flourish, and now they grow horizontally, refuting the very essence of "tree." A tree's job is to be tall, and these are, well, *wide*.

We paddle for only ten minutes or so before Mark shouts up to me, saying dig for the shore here, and we do, bearing down hard on the port side of the canoe. We swing against the current and easily cut through it, coming to a red-clay riverbank, where there is nearly sickening evidence of our own kind—a cracked Styrofoam cooler, a couple of drained beer cans, and a hundred footprints of yesterday's fishermen. On this Friday midmorning, however, no one is about, and we pull the canoe up and tie its bow rope to a tree.

"I haven't been here in a long time, either," I say. "How far are we?"

"We're right here," he says. "Just up there."

And we walk through a clearing and come quickly to an area we can see has been well kept. My eyes follow the stunning sight before us: the ruins of the ghost town of Scull Shoals, now a well-maintained locale called the Scull Shoals Historical Recreation Area. Often, there are visitors here—from University of Georgia students studying historical preservation to ecology to kids on field trips—but this morning, the place is utterly silent. We could have just come off the Missouri with Lewis and Clark.

Mark and I have known about this place for years, but this is his land, not mine. Our friend Caroline Hunt, a local historian in Madison, wrote a history of the vanished town many years before and did a very fine job of it. Caroline was our parents' age, and now she is gone, but her work will endure.

This was the frontier in 1782 when settlers pushed from Savannah to Augusta and then on into the unsettled heart of Georgia. Less than fifty years had passed since James Edward Oglethorpe and a group of settlers arrived to found Savannah where the Savannah River empties into the Atlantic Ocean. Even though the local Native Americans had moved west and north of here by the late 1700s for reasons we don't really know, they still hunted here, and parties of them harassed the settlers of Scull Shoals until they finally built a fort to protect themselves in 1796. These were Creeks and possibly others—Native Americans ranged widely, and such distant tribes as Mohawks sometimes visited the Cherokees of northwestern South Carolina, not 75 miles from here.

In 1802, the Creeks gave up, ceding these and adjacent lands, continuing the sad pullback across America that would result in genocide later in the century. That the settlers didn't know any better is no excuse. We came, we saw, we conquered. With the Native Americans gone, and with cotton farming now profitable because of Eli Whitney's cotton gin, settlers began to pour into this upcountry.

At Scull Shoals, they built the requisite cotton gin, plus a sawmill and a gristmill. George Paschal and Zachariah Sims built a paper mill here in 1811, but it didn't last long. (As a writer, I have to marvel at the very idea: a paper mill less than a decade after the last Indian had moved.)

Caroline Hunt's history is excerpted in a website maintained by the Friends of Scull Shoals.

"Under its third owner, Dr. Thomas Poullain, Sr., there were flourishing mills, boarding houses, stores, a warehouse, distillery, a toll bridge, and other enterprises. In 1854, for example, he had 2000 spindles and looms.... Dr. Lindsay Durham was an early community leader. He had a large herb garden and developed patented medicines that he and his medical family used to treat their patients. Durham's 60-bed hospital was in cabins scattered around his home. It was a major facility for the time. The village was also the home to Georgia governor Peter Early."

In 1845, fire, unstoppable in frame buildings even with a river close by, burned much of Scull Shoals. To replace the burned-out hulls, people built three-and four-story brick buildings. In 1887, a flood left water standing throughout the town for four days. In the late 1880s, the town's covered bridge was washed off downstream in a flood. The cotton in the warehouse was destroyed, and the town never quite came back from that disaster.

In the century of white habitation, farmers had managed what Native Americans had not in several thousand years: They ruined the land for agriculture. Monocropping cotton was disastrous, and the shallow topsoil, plowed years after year, simply bled off into the river and floated away. The soil was useless. Families, unable to grow cotton, moved to larger towns such as Athens farther upriver. The mills had all closed by 1900. The scrap iron and brick from the buildings was torn down over the years for sale, leaving nothing. The last residents were gone by 1935.

"Today," the website continues, "only three walls of the warehouse and store remain standing, along with the arched bridge that took workers across the raceway into the mills. Between 1875 and 1930, the land was sold several times. Then, in the 1930's, it was reassembled and sold to the government for an experimental forest. The Soil Conservation Service and Civilian Conservation Corps did massive reclamations, terracing eroded hillsides and replanting the forests. Scull Shoals became part of the Oconee National Forest in 1949.... in 1996, the Friends of Scull Shoals was chartered, and efforts expanded to study the history of this once-important industrial center in the middle Georgia piedmont."

So many people, so many mornings—and now, the silence of crumbled walls. Mark and I walk among them, admiring the excellent upkeep of the site. A considerable amount of archaeology has now been done on this site, too, principally by Forest Service archaeologist Jack Wynn (who has worked at the site for more than twenty years) and dozens of well-trained volunteers. They are peeling back time. Other volunteers have begun to compile oral histories, recording the stories of the very old and last living residents of the town.

Still, something melancholy hangs in the air this morning, a sense of loss and futility, that for anyone who lives on a river, the next rainstorm can bring disaster. This feeling is reinforced by the quiet buzzing of insects, the slow flakes of butterflies as they skip from petal to petal. After fifteen minutes walking through the ruins of Scull Shoals, I'm ready to leave these "ghostly demarcations" for "keener sounds."

Mark and I push the canoe back into the current of the
Oconee River, and by now the morning is edging toward
noon, the point at which, for me, daily life begins to
collapse upon itself. As many people despise morning, I
find afternoons almost intolerable, with their creeping
hours, dull light, and lack of an edge. We are a smooth
team now, almost dried from our spill a few hours earlier,
and we dig the water with practiced strokes, easily steering
the canoe through water whose average depth is probably
no more than 3 feet.

For a time, we hear the sound of a chainsaw, but we
never see a man bearing one. Then another motor, perhaps
a rogue four-wheeler ripping up the floodplain. After that,
all we hear are natural sounds, birdsong, the sweet hiss of
river water, and wind in the oaks and elms. The river flows
straight for a time, and then breaks off in a sharp bend to
starboard. The *ca-luink* of leaping and falling fish is all
around us, and I look down and see beneath us swiftly
swimming bass, and a few logy catfish. We bump bottom a
few times but manage to stay afloat

Great washes of alluvium have moved into this river
over the centuries, a kind of poor-man's tectonic plate, but
despite humankind's best efforts to destroy the land, nature
has reclaimed it, as if to say, *You blew it once; don't do it a
second time.* Given human pride and stupidity (such as the
desire to drill up the remaining wilderness rather than
conserve one paint bucket worth of oil), one wonders how
many chances we will get.

Unlike Lake Oconee, which can be raised or
artificially drawn down, the river obeys its geology and the
area's rainfall patterns. In flood, the river swells like a

molten monster, elbowing its way back up Wildcat Creek, which drains into the Oconee barely half a mile from my house. While the river here is 3 feet deep now, I've seen the creek below my house 12 feet deep after a week's rain, meaning the river is probably twice that.

Yet the area's riverine biome is the same, and the trees, base plants, fish, mammals are the same here they are in the rest of my country. With exceptions.

We have been on the river now for several hours, and trip has been exhilarating, perfect. I have exulted in the morning, and already I'm sad to think soon we will take out at the Forest Service campground near the Highway 15 bridge. I dig along in the water, and sometimes we pass places 5, 6 feet deep, but always we come right back to our 3-foot bottom. The river is not straight—there are bends and incipient oxbows, and often we take sweeping curves that the river began making around rock formations millennia before. I am wondering how far we have left when I see heaven through the canopy, about 40 degrees off the ground.

"My God, *look*!" I cry, and I take the paddle, place it across my lap and see my hand rise, almost as if it were part of some other man. There, swooping over us with the glare of an emperor, is a bald eagle, clearly fishing in the shallow waters, banking, angling, coveting the shape of the morning light. It is breathtaking, not only for the raptor's inherent majesty but because I've lived in this land all my life and never seen one.

The irony, of course, is that they are only here because of the manmade lake a few miles downstream.

"Damn!" says Mark. "Right here on our own river!"

"A bald eagle," I say, barely believing it, my voice falling. I have quit paddling, but the canoe doesn't seem to care, and it still slips easily straight down the river. Mark removes his paddle, too, and we are silent, and the eagle cuts once back through the canopy in the light, but the bird has moved away from us, gone. But it *was* there: the nation's bird, wearing morning on its 5-foot wingspan like a cloak of gold.

We say nothing for a time and then begin to paddle again. Twenty minutes later, Mark says we're not far from the paved boat put-in at the Forest Service campground, and as always, he's worried about mastery.

"It's easy to miss a single spot coming off a river," he says. "I've seen people in canoes heading for a take-out just fly right on past it and have to turn around and try to paddle against the current. It's embarrassing."

"I'm with you," I say.

And there it is, 200 yards ahead, and campers are walking on the riverbank, and a couple of kids even stand at the very spot we have to get out. Like a team of Percherons, however, we dig stolidly and with perfect synchrony. And we cut across the current and come straight into the slip without a mishap. I climb out first in ankle deep water and pull the canoe up onto the paved area, then turn to see my brother grinning.

The last light of morning spangles his great gray and brown beard, and he's laughing.

Morning is a marker for our lives as well as a time. The history of people and places, of vanished Indians and ghost towns—all these had their mornings, too, and my kinship to them is more than one of place and topography. I feel a whispered edge of the ineffable as well, a brotherhood of mornings.

History's Mornings

Our past has been shaped by events of the morning. These may be no more than accidents of history, but often I wonder why certain things happen at specific times in the day.

Each June, I celebrate the day of Custer's Massacre at the Little Big Horn. I celebrate it for the howling joy I feel in his defeat, the last high watermark for Native Americans in their fight against whites' move west. Custer, earlier, had led his troops in what laughably came to be called the Battle of the Washita, when he attacked a sleeping village at dawn in the snow. General George Crook did the same thing in the run-up to the Custer fight. It takes a real man to shoot a woman or a child in the predawn cold.

My feelings about American Indian history come naturally, for when I was a boy, my father took my brother and me into the great Keowee Valley in northwestern South Carolina, and that land was the trailway of empires. We tramped the land and played in the river, which poured straight from the mountains, cold and clear over water-smooth stones.

History in that land shaped itself, also, around a morning, this one on February 16, 1760.

Then the land there was glorious—a river as picturesque as any in America, bubbling through the foothills of the Great Smoky Mountains. The bottomland was incredibly fertile, and for more than 2000 years at least,

Indians had lived here, growing crops, killing game, taking fish. My first visit to the valley is lost in the veil of early childhood, but we went frequently because of my father's obsession with Native Americans and with his own homeland. He and my mother both grew up in another Oconee County—this one in South Carolina, which was to the west of the Keowee River. Across it to the east is Pickens County.

On the Oconee County side there was a large Cherokee Indian village called Keowee, one of several of the so-called Lower Towns, a once-flourishing empire of accomplished and intelligent people whose land stretched northwestward more than 100 miles into the high mountains. In 1753, the British, at the request of the Cherokees, built a fort across the river on what is now the Pickens County side—Fort Prince George. It was a standard British military outpost—a small square fort with elongated, diamond-shaped bastions.

Those were parlous times, with alliances shifting constantly between Indian tribes, between the French and the British, between South Carolinians and Virginians. Fearful of attacks, the Lower Cherokees asked for a fort, which the British were only too happy to build. In those days, this was the true frontier, as alien to soldiers and settlers as the West would be to Lewis and Clark nearly half a century later.

There were long stretches of peace, but by the time of the French and Indian War the area was a battlefield, and though there were a few traders and soldiers who knew and understood the life of the Cherokees, most couldn't understand why they didn't act like proper British citizens.

Like all good stories, there was a villain in this one, and his name was Lt. Richard Coytmore, a vain and stupid

commander who had taken over Ft. Prince George during
the war. Worse than his vanity (which was huge) was his
arrogance and his belief that the Indians, to use the
common parlance of the eighteenth and nineteenth
centuries, were savages. So when I think of the attacks at
dawn in the Western Indian wars, I see a delicious irony of
the events of February 16, 1760.

Times were terrible for everyone. The fort was full of
disease, and the village of Keowee was in a bad way.
Fighting had been going on for months, and the
Cherokees, naked and freezing, did not know whom to
trust. They knew well enough, however, that Coytmore's
presence was disastrous. Not long before, he had been
spotted during a dance in Keowee, drunk and making fun
of the Indians. And his manner, even according to reports
of his own men, was brusque and even cruel.

This morning, the great Cherokee chief Oconostota
sent word that he wanted to see Coytmore at the ford in
the river. Disgusted at having to be awakened on a cold,
snowy morning, one in which fog lay on the river,
Coytmore roused himself and walked the few hundred
yards from the fort to the river with an Ensign Bell; a
trader, Cornelius Dougherty; and a translator named
Forster.

Oconostota was on the Keowee side of the river, and
he shouted something out in Cherokee, which Forster
translated as "I want a white man to go with me to town,"
meaning Charles Town, which was several hundred miles
to the south. Relieved, Coytmore told Forster, "Tell him if
that's all he wants I will get somebody to go with him."

"Then I will catch a horse!" cried Oconostota. At that
point, the chief whirled a bridle around his head, and shots
rang out from the underbrush along the river. Bell took a

bullet in the calf, and Forster got it in the ass, which leaves no doubt about which way he was headed. Coytmore took a bullet through a lung, which from 50 or 60 yards away has to be counted a fine shot with a smoothbore musket.

The others dragged Coytmore back to the fort, where he managed to live for a while before expiring. After his death, soldiers massacred Indian hostages in the fort, one of the stunning, and virtually unknown, events in American history. The soldiers hacked unarmed men to bits.

That morning changed the history of the frontier. Whatever justice the Cherokees saw in killing Coytmore, his death, like the Battle of the Little Bighorn, was ultimately a pyrrhic victory.

Flash forward to another morning, 208 years later. For weeks, crews have been cutting down all the trees in the glorious Keowee Valley because the Duke Power Company, damn their eyes, is about to impound a lake that will flood the area with water a hundred feet deep.

I am eighteen years old, and Mark, our father, and I have been working for months, when we have time, as volunteers with an archaeologist from the University of South Carolina who is racing the calendar to excavate Fort Prince George. The valley, one of the most beautiful in the Southern United States, has been destroyed. I feel literally sick every time I see it, and I know Mark and our father do, too. I have come to think of the 1960s as America's Last Period of Gullibility, when it could be over-awed by utility companies to such an extent they would allow their heritage to be raped. People know about this mostly from the West, but it happened all over the South, too.

We have no time for polemics, though. It's early on a foggy spring morning, and we have already uncovered the clear outlines of the fort, bastions and all. We have found the skeleton of a man who we believe is Lt. Coytmore. We know his body was buried inside the fort, and it's the only such burial here. Looking on his skeleton, laid out neatly, I feel a shudder of sorrow for the man and his stupidities. *What is man, that Thou are mindful of him?* Lt. Richard Coytmore may have been many things, but I have serious doubts that he was but "a little lower than the angels."

Our job this morning, however, involves a stone building, whose gray mass we discovered fairly early in the excavations. Hundreds of years ago, the building collapsed, and someone, probably a farmer, pushed all the stone into the building's cellar and covered it over with topsoil for farming. Generations planted crops right on top of Coytmore and this structure without really knowing it. (Local legend had never lost the location of the fort, however, even though no one had really studied it in the two centuries since it fell or was pulled down.)

The fog lies heavily on the river this morning, an omen for those inclined to see them. We have decided to empty the building's foundation of its stones, most the size of a medicine ball and weighing perhaps 30 or 40 pounds each. We have to take the rocks, once a wall in a British colonial fort building, about 100 yards away, past the outlines of the fort to a spot near the existing road. We do not know what we will find at the bottom of the rocks, but the feeling of the crew is not unlike that of Lord Carnarvon and Howard Carter in Egypt's Valley of the Kings in fall 1922.

I have learned, on this dig, to use a whiskbroom or a paintbrush to clean around the most delicate of artifacts—the base of a rum jug, an iron drainage grate, the stem of a wineglass. Today's job is grunt work, however, and we take turns with it. Wearing thick work gloves, we remove the rocks from the cellar and place them in heavy construction wheelbarrows. For a long time, I pick up rocks and toss them into the wide-mawed barrows, where they hit with a muffled thud. I look toward the river, a lovely place I have known intimately for more than a decade, and see the trees gone, the landscape as blasted and barren as Mars. Over the years, I will have ample opportunity to forgive and forget, to see the deep blue waters of Lake Keowee and know the pleasure they bring thousands. I will never forget, though, and I cannot forgive. If one can commit genocide upon the land, this is it.

The air is heavy this morning, almost stunned. Mark will go on to be an archaeologist, and I will become a novelist, poet, and science writer—legacies of these mornings along a condemned valley. There is a rumor of sun. Often, it comes cutting through these low clouds with cinematic grandeur, sending shafts of light into the valley. I do not have to imagine why the Cherokees loved this land, and the irony that white men first drove them out and then destroyed it all is too sickening to ponder.

My turn has come for wheelbarrow duty. We switch places, and I begin trundling the back-straining loads of stone through the fort, past the outer walls, over what was once a moat, and to the edge of the road. Sadly, no official report will ever be written on Fort Prince George, though thirty years later, my father will pen a marvelous monograph that is part history and part memoir.

The work is dull and long. Despite the fact that the morning is very cool, I am soon sweating through my clothes but enjoying the pull of stone against muscle. It is not yet midmorning, and the sun begins to tear the clouds apart. The fog isn't quite ready to dissolve, though, clinging to the river bottom as it has for millennia, and I find myself wishing the mist were sentient, able to understand that its own days are numbered.

I drone on, and on perhaps my fifteenth wheelbarrow load of rocks from the cellar, I turn it up with a groan, and just then, the sun spikes through the clouds and fog, and it cuts along a rock I have just turned over. The rock has landed *just-so*, and on its surface there appear to be markings of some kind. I inhale sharply. The sun reveals numbers deeply etched on the simple stone surface.

I reach for it with my gloved hand and brush it off, and it appears to be the numbers 194 and another digit. My first thought: This must be some kind of geodesic marker placed here during the WWII years, but then I realize that's impossible. Nineteen Forty-*what?* I brush harder and then, with my breath growing ragged, I lift the rock and gently turn it over. It's not very large, perhaps 12 or 15 pounds. The sunlight knocks a river of knowledge into me. It is a full and clear date that has been carved into the rock: *1761.* I begin walking back toward the others, straight into the sunlight, and I can't get my breath.

Oh, my God, I think, *It's the cornerstone.* Now, halfway to the fort's heart, I see another date in smaller, less-certain carving just below it: 1770, and I register another event that happened that year, one I would know well enough in my classical-music-rich household: the year of Beethoven's birth half a world away.

By the time I get back, my hands are shaking, the morning has ripped back the shroud of fog in the Keowee Valley, and I say the only thing that I can blurt out: "I've found something. You better come look at this." The others climb out of the cellar and come slowly to me, not expecting much but grateful for a small break in the aching labor.

"I don't believe it!" my father cries when he sees it. Mark is jubilant. The others whack me on the back, crow and shout. I don't know how Howard Carter felt exactly when he first peered into Tutankhamen's tomb, but I have a good idea, one that will stay with me all my life. The strange fortune of archaeology has uncovered an artifact that by all rules should never have been discovered.

Two things conspired: Sheer luck and sun tearing the mist into meteorological wreckage. We take a coffee break and admire the cornerstone and talk excitedly about the discovery, about history, about salvage archaeology. For years after that, we will relive the moment, and I will hone the story in my telling, the way Cherokees refined their stories for hundreds of years.

The rock, of course, was taken to the archaeological collections at the University of South Carolina, and I have never seen it again, though I have a spectacular photograph of it taken that morning by my father. The morning light is full and strong upon the year 1761.

⊱—

Another morning, thirty-two years later. Mark and I have passed fifty, and our father, still vigorous as he nears eighty. We are driving to the Keowee-Toxaway Visitor's Center, which lies at the upper end of Lake Keowee. We are going to see our father's scale model of Ft. Prince George, which he built more than two decades before and has now donated to the center, which was built to focus on the area's natural and human history. It was a nice gesture, but one that makes up for only one ten-thousandth of the damage done.

The entire glorious Keowee Valley went under water in May 1968, and our father was one of the few people—if not the only one—to see its demise. He drove to a spot in the hills high above the valley and watched as the waters spilled from the Keowee River and flowed over the site of the fort, the village of Keowee, and the ford where Lt. Coytmore had been shot. A veteran of the Army Air Corps in WWII, he stood ramrod straight and gave his best military salute as the valley died.

I don't think the three of us ever got over it. We will all carry to our graves an enduring disgust with dam-building projects and a love for wilderness and history. But hatred is a corrosive emotion, and in my calmer hours, I can admit that the lake is gorgeous, that it supplies power, and that nature itself changes the natural world as much as man has. These are feelings that are forced from my soul by a desire for fairness, however. The truth is indelible. What we lost with the construction of this lake was incalculable.

This morning summer has settled its strong humid warmth over the South, but even when we park and get out, the air here, in the far northwestern corner of South Carolina, is almost sweet enough to sip through a straw. The Visitor's Center needs some work, but it's reasonably well maintained. A succession of small buildings tumbles through the woods with clots of rhododendron and mountain laurel as neighbors. In each building there is a display of history, along with artifacts, artwork, and written descriptions of the area's history.

We come to the building housing my father's fort, and there it is. We remember the incredible care he took in building it to absolute scale, making well-educated guesses when we weren't sure of some facts. (The outlines of the buildings were clear enough during our excavations, and we easily found the well in the center of the fort. We dug it down as far as we dared, and Mark, always more courageous than I, allowed himself to be lowered far down into the hole to look for artifacts. Alas, the water table on the river was obviously high, and we never found the well's bottom.)

There's no sentimentality here. We cast a careful eye on the fort's condition, and it's certainly far better than what the real fort endured during its twenty-odd years of life. There are the few stray roach husks, and that irritates our father, who put untold hours of work into the model. This is a serious contribution to the history of the area, but no casual observer of the display would have a clue of our years in the Keowee Valley and how our knowledge of the fort changed that foggy morning I found a single stone.

I walk past them as we head back toward the car, hiking slowly up the sharp slopes in the luxurious shade. The morning is thick with the hidden nets of spiders, and I walk face-first into them and turn into a swatting thing. Few others are about, even though it's a sunny Saturday. Most people would be out there on the lake with their expensive boats, their noises, amid the fog of burning diesel.

Does history make distinctions among the ticks of daylight? There have been innumerable battles at dawn, but the percentage overall, among history's wars, is small. In the American Civil War, there were battles that raged long after dark, but fewer that began at dawn. Far more often, battles ended with retreats at dawn.

I was reading the *New York Times* online one morning in September 2001 when a bulletin flashed that a plane had struck one of the towers of the World Trade Center. I had been in those towers as perhaps millions had over the past twenty-five years. Did the terrorists calculate that security forces would be less alert, less willing to believe such carnage possible *in the morning*? Did they count on the slow awakening of America to abet their evil?

I don't believe this is a silly speculation. Possibilities are different in the morning to a person with a manic will. A man who is a coward at midnight will find courage or the full-bloom of madness with dawn. For every Battle of the Washita, there are ten Little Big Horns, fought in the heat of a summer day.

We can imagine nighttime ceremonies atop the mound at Scull Shoals, fires burning, and the sound of singing, of praising the river and the night and the morning. We can hear the sounds of the gristmill at the town there as it began to roar for the day. And it takes only a little thought to penetrate the scene in which Lt. Coytmore was shot at the ford in the Keowee River just below Fort Prince George.

History covets its mornings, but we await the historian who will write that saga.

Morning's Third Sense:
The Aroma of Dawn

High autumn has arrived on Wildcat Ridge, and the white oaks are a profusion of bronze and siennas. The dogwoods have gone candy-apple red, and the leaves of beech trees that stand with their thick-chested majesty by the creek are yellow as banana skins.

I love the smell of morning this time of year. But morning doesn't have its own odor, you say, and you'd probably be right. But like many things we construct in our thinking as humans, we have developed an aroma of morning.

When I was small, we went to church, and one morning a month, the men of the congregation had a breakfast in the large room off which our Sunday school classes were located. When I walked inside, the smell of just-cooked bacon and eggs, of freshly brewed coffee and crisp toast made me ravenous. That smell *was* morning to me.

Years later, when we were camping, I would always be the first to arise and get the fire going again, and soon I'd have water boiling. I could *taste* the lake, fishy and rich with hydrilla and dissolved organic material, and the coffee would spread its lovely scent through the tent as my wife and son rose and stumbled with the primal urgings of food.

Human smells are one thing, but the Earth's awakening at morning is something else entirely. The new warmth of sunlight causes a billion organic engines in these woods to start cranking up for the day. If I sit on the Philosopher's Stones and breathe in the pleasant rot of roots and animals that is one kind of sensation. But if I kneel in the new sunlight and lower my face to the leaf litter, that is something else entirely.

So here I am kneeling, for science and supplication. The first thing I do is break a small red-capped mushroom open and hold it to my nostrils. No amanita, nothing poison, this small fungal trophy emits the same smell you take from any salad-bar mushroom—slight, earthy, yet somehow memorable. Is it different in the morning or would it smell the same at midnight?

The probable issue is that *I* am different in the morning. What if a mushroom in the forest emits its earthy smell, and no one is there to smell it? Even so, in the season of autumn, as leaves pour down around me like a brown-and-yellow stream, there is some different quality to the aroma of morning.

I am smelling the mushroom when I am taken back to another place, another morning.

＊

For several years, I drove, long before dawn on Sunday mornings, to the Sandy Creek Nature Center north of Athens. This center, which consists of trails, an interpretative building, and a small pond, is a place of delight and has long been a retreat for the town-bound who rarely see nature as we do in the country.

In those days, we lived on a dead-end street in a small subdivision, and I was a newspaper editor. The stress of newspaper work had me manic and edgy by the weekend, and I would worship in the cathedral of dark limbs as I walked on moonlight trails to the pond to fish.

Those were days of glory. I arrived, especially on autumn days, at the padlocked gate that was perhaps half a mile from the interpretative building. Trails spread from that location, and I knew them well. I arrived by five and took my rod and my tackle box and began the slow walk through the forest toward the Clay Pit Pond.

This odd name came from the fact that a brick factory flourished on the site in the nineteenth century, and workers took clay from the low area and used it in the kilns. The aroma of pinewoods, of the needled forest floor, of the lake, of an east wind—they all come back when I think of those days.

Those mornings were transcendent, God-filled. I was completely alone, and though I could see an occasional car on the road several hundred yards through the canopy, the only sounds and smells came from the forest and the pond. Once, walking down the sloping trail in the darkness, I stopped to listen. Great-horned owls spoke to each other. Something small and stealthy and four-legged crept through the brush. I sat and felt the Earth's inheritance in my veins.

Then I smelled it: several hundred yards distant, Clay Pit Pond sent its aroma upward toward me on a breeze, and the pond smelled like fish. (Seasoned fishermen say they can smell when a lake is ripe with fish, and I've shared that sensation myself.) I was in no hurry though. The fish—bream, catfish, carp, and an occasional bass—had nowhere else to go.

Did humankind ever navigate by smell? Of course. Perhaps it was the whiff of a council fire or roasting meat. Most Indian villages, to our twenty-first century noses, would have probably smelled terrible and been obvious from quite a distance. (When a village site became too foul, Native Americans would simply move the whole village to a newer site. Smart people.) I imagine, too, hunters coming back from a long trail and smelling Lake Huron or the Mississippi or even Wildcat Creek. Farming Indians would have smelled rain coming and praised it.

That day, I was trying to steer my way through the woods by smell alone, too. I wondered: If I close my eyes, can I find the pond simply by the intensity of its odors? It was a silly surmise, since the pond lay in a natural basin, and you have to walk downhill to reach it. I would have to be a complete idiot to go in the wrong direction.

Morning was not far away. Already, I could see my own hand. The idea each Sunday morning was to reach the pond at first light. The sight of my 8-pound-test line unspooling from the reel at dawn filled me with something near rapture. This morning, though, I dawdled on the trail. I did not want the hardships of life from centuries before. Even then, in my early thirties, I loved the comfort of an air-conditioned room in summer, a soft bed, and a book-lined study. Still, I wanted the Native Americans' connection to the Earth, with all its affections and horrors.

I closed my eyes and stood and walked toward the smell of the pond. Feet, however, rely on eyes for navigation, not noses, and soon I tripped on a root and fell headlong into a clutch of briars. It took me a long while to get loose, and I was torn and bleeding as I cursed myself and went on toward the pond.

Then, as if to grant grace to fools, the sun rose enough to shed light on the surface of the pond, and a delicious odor washed over me. I knew I would catch all I wanted for breakfast that day. On my first cast, I watched the line in the low light, sharply inhaling at its flowing beauty. As the bait hit the water—*bam*. A bream struck it and took off running. Near the pond's center, a beaver watched me with what seemed like amused interest.

I reeled in the prize, a palm-sized redbreast that would feed me a few hours later, and I held it to my nose and smelled its richness. I remember those mornings principally now for their odors, and those odors stayed on me so that when I arrived home, Linda sent me to the shower after I cleaned the fish.

If one odor is most closely associated with morning, it's that from coffee. That's a no-brainer. We may argue and fight over oil and where America should obtain it, but most people don't care. (People *do* care about drilling our sensitive ecological areas, which right-wingers want to do with a vengeance.) If we ran out of oil, someone in short order would invent cars with efficient solar engines. But heaven help us if we ran out of coffee.

You want to see a fight, turn off the coffee spigot.

A columnist for the *Minneapolis Star-Tribune*, James Lileks, in 1997 asked his readers for morning rituals.

"…I expected to get vignettes along these lines," he wrote: "'No morning is complete without a buttery croissant savored in the sun room, while the children— dressed in their Von Trapp costumes, arranged by height—

hum Vivaldi quartets from a respectful distance. Then it's off to the keno parlor.'"

What he got, in fact, was a considerable amount of undisguised bitching. One reader said the greatest problem was that you need coffee to be able to wake up enough to make coffee. Many readers spoke about the snooze bar on their alarm clocks. One man said his significant other hits her snooze bar about four times in the morning. "If I want to be bothered every seven minutes, I would have another child," he wrote.

Another reader said his life was a "series of random events strung loosely together. I don't exactly have a ritual in the morning; however, I'll often try to do 50 sit-ups, feed my cats, and shave every morning. These are done in no particular order."

Lileks suggests, to vary things, he might try shaving the cats.

The aroma of a shower: soap, shampoo, and city water smelling of iron filings. For men (and sometimes women), shaving cream and aftershave or some kind of cooling balm.

Then it's to the kitchen where the coffee might have dripped or perked by then. A few minutes later, you get the screeching smell of a burned bagel and the pleasure of cream cheese or margarine. I spent many mornings smelling my children's forays into Fruit Loops or Count Chocula.

I'm beginning to see why there have been so few books about morning. Most people, it seems, set their clocks ten minutes ahead, hit the snooze bar repeatedly, and then rise with the élan of a moose stranded on a frozen lake. I have never used an alarm clock at all. I awake every day between 4:15 and 4:30, wide awake and ready to roll.

When I tell people this, they often back away from me, as if I have something like typhus that may be catching.

The best description in literature of the smells of morning—in all their glory and grossness—is from James Joyce's great novel *Ulysses*. This is my take-to-the-desert-island book. It is funny, brilliant, and so acute that you feel in the presence of the stuffy and guilt-ridden Stephen Dedalus or the wonderfully human Leopold Bloom.

The novel opens with Dedalus and his friend Buck Mulligan standing on the parapet of the decommissioned defense tower where they live in Dublin. Mulligan is holding a "bowl of lather" for shaving—and in that sharp morning light, you can almost smell it.

After talking for a while and shaving, Stephen remembers his mother's death. In a dream after she had died, she appeared to him "giving off an odor of wax and rosewood," and her breath had "a faint odor of wetted ashes." A few moments later, he recalls his mother's life: "Her glass of water from the kitchen tap when she had approached the sacrament. A cored apple, filled with brown sugar, roasting for her at the hob on a dark autumn evening."

Stephen and Buck go back down the stairs, ignoring the stench of coal smoke, into the living quarters where their friend Haines is coming around after bad dreams of a panther. Now it's time for breakfast, and in short order, Joyce writes of tea, lemon, bread, butter, honey, and milk.

But this is nothing compared to our first glimpse of Leopold Bloom in chapter 4, which corresponds to the

"Calypso" section in the *Odyssey*. The chapter's opening paragraph is a classic of taste and smell:

"Mr Leopold Bloom ate with relish the inner organs of beasts and fowls. He liked thick giblet soup, nutty gizzards, a stuffed roast heart, liverslices fried with crustcrumbs, friend hencods' roes. Most of all he liked grilled mutton kidneys which gave to his palate a fine tang of faintly scented urine."

Joyce thus deftly combines images of breakfast and bathroom—something he will do with even more obvious and classic grossness a while later. He mentions ham, pepper, eggs, butter, tea, bread, and potatoes in the space of a couple of paragraphs. Bloom checks on his wife, Molly, who hates morning and is barely coherent. Then he takes a stroll and buys a fresh kidney and a pound and a half of sausage for their breakfast. The scent almost rises off the pages.

Once home, he unwraps the kidney while his cat is rubbing on his legs, mad for the smell of meat. Bloom puts the kidney in a frying pan with melted butter while the cat hungrily licks the paper. He peppers the kidney while it sizzles in the butter.

The tea is ready by now, as is the bread and butter. He takes breakfast to Molly and in a bit eats his own meal, dipping his bread in the kidney-butter sauce. The mail has come, and he reads a letter from his daughter, Milly—the equivalent today of checking e-mail and reading the *New York Times* online before heading for work.

Then—for what might have been the first time in fiction—Bloom retires to the outhouse in a scene where almost nothing is left to the imagination. Even there, in morning smell that poets have ignored for two thousand years, Bloom stops to regard some spearmint growing nearby.

The entire novel is a sensual feast, but these twin morning scenes and their breakfast and human smells are indelible. They are who we are.

If autumn in our forest has its own smell, so do the other seasons. Often in winter I'll catch a whiff of wood smoke from a neighbor's fireplace or leaf burning. In summer when there's an unyielding temperature inversion, we can sometimes smell chicken houses being cleaned out several miles away. Spring is the time of rain on the warming earth, delicious and nourishing.

Today, though, in the world of autumn, there is something reminiscent of curing time in the old days—leaves curling and sere. I pick up a handful of broad white oak leaves, brown and dead, and crumble them in my hands and hold them close under my nose. Yes, I think: boyhood seasons of raking and leaping into piles of fall.

I am trying to think, though, if any of our natural smells on the ridge are peculiar to morning. What kind of instruments could begin to know? That's one of the main problems with writing about morning from anything approaching scientific rigor: Nobody has cared enough about the whole concept to spend much time investigating it.

Can you imagine writing a grant proposal to the National Science Foundation asking for support to study whether morning smells differently from night? I asked a number of people I know if morning has its own peculiar smell, and, like James Lileks's respondents, they looked at me as if I'd lost my mind. The only thing most of them want to smell is coffee, preferably coffee made by someone else. I shudder to think what the divorce rate would be without coffee.

I can't prove that morning has its own inimical set of natural aromas, but I believe it. People have been fighting wars for thousands of years over things they can't prove. I see no harm in asserting that morning is more complex than a snooze bar and three cups of coffee.

The Mornings of One Man's Life

I love the writing of Edward Abbey, whose beloved Southwest desert is not my country but which intrigues me nonetheless. He was Pennsylvania-born but chose to live his life elsewhere. I have spent my life, except for one six-month span, within 30 miles of the spot where I was born.

In his great book *Desert Solitaire*, Abbey writes of one morning when he began his work as a ranger in Arches National Monument in southeastern Utah. Like all of us, he makes coffee first, then he sits and waits for the sun to rise. His description is classic Abbey.

"Suddenly it comes, the flaming globe, blazing on the pinnacles and minarets and balanced rocks, on the canyon walls and through the windows in the sandstone fins. We greet each other, sun and I, across the black void of ninety-three million miles."

Faced with such writing, I want simply to nod. Abbey is brilliant at making readers feel precisely what he sees. My own mornings, when I spread them across America, have their own aromas and flavors as well.

Key West, 1970

I am sitting on the deck of a rented houseboat on the flat expanse of Florida Bay, the shallow water between the end of mainland Florida and the Keys. The evening before, I caught, cooked, and devoured, a large red snapper, and this morning, my friends are still asleep below-deck as I stand at the bow's starboard rail and look across the fog-spread waters.

So far, the sun is only a rumor. The plunk of a fish, retreating into water after having come up to spy upon the air, resounds deeply. Seabirds glide over the surface of the water, coming by like silent-movie ice skaters. The fog begins to lift in small cloudbanks, undulating upward.

I feel a shuddering terror in the pre-dawn. The day before, we had been exploring the John Pennekamp Coral Reef State Park south of Key Largo, and I had come as close to Death as I want to get without being on speaking terms with him. Another morning, but now it seems millennia past. We had anchored and leaped into the 5 foot water to snorkel and look at coral formations that grace the area.

In late morning, when the heat of July was rising upon the face of the waters, I had managed to slice my foot on a coral formation, and it had blossomed with blood. I cursed, swam back to the boat, and bandaged my foot and put on sneakers, re-entered the waters.

I could stay beneath the water, goggle-bound, for a very long time, rising just high enough to blow out my snorkel, inhale fresh salty air, and dive again. I stayed longer and longer beneath the water, and on one final dive, I was down for perhaps fifteen minutes, exulting in the subtle colors and shapes of coral and the shaft of morning light through the shallow water.

I rose again to blow out my snorkel and inhale fresh air, when I managed to suck in some water and came up into the sunlight for a long breath of air. The water was only up to my chin. I smelled it first, then saw it: *blood*. Quarts of blood, *barrels* of blood. And the others screaming at me. I whirled as well I could in my waterlogged sneakers, but I could tell my own foot was bleeding again. A single word roared over and over from the boat like spoken semaphore:

Shark! Shark! Shark!

I knew I was going to die, just before my sophomore year in college. I looked around slowly, and a dark dorsal fin cut through the water not 10 feet from me, and in its wake bobbed half of a 5-foot-long tarpon, its tail and a large part of its middle bitten cleanly off. I stood in the middle of its spilled blood, which floated on the surface of the water like oil.

The shark fed furiously, gnashing the tarpon's tail like a light hors d'oeuvre, and I could now see, from the span between its dorsal and tail fins, that it was at least 12 feet long. This was in the days before Peter Benchley's novel *Jaws* or the movie made from it. (Oddly enough, years later Richard Zanuck and David Brown, the producers of *Jaws*, would option film rights from one of my novels and keep them for many seasons.) Still, I knew I was in terrible danger, and I looked toward escape.

The mangrove-lined shore was probably half a mile away. Our houseboat bobbed several hundred yards behind me in the Gulf of Mexico. I remembered well enough what you do *not* do around a shark: thrash and make a lot of noise. So here I was, in the middle of a spreading pool of blood, wearing sneakers. The shark came up then, and I could see his blood-drenched mouth and the 3-inch-long teeth and his wild, dead eyes.

And behind me two words now: my own name and the name of my killer.

My mind simply turned off. I fell to my chest and inhaled a mouthful of tarpon blood and began to swim toward the boat. I was only an adequate swimmer, for I have never been strong, fast, or even athletic. But at that moment, I felt like Johnny Weismuller, tennis shoes and all. The blood in my mouth was potent, salty. I imagined the shark swallowing the last of the tarpon's tailfin and heading for me. My friends screamed and ran from one end of the boat to the other. I could not breathe, but I swam anyway.

The closer I came to the boat, the more fearful I was. In the movie *Jaws*, the character Quint, played by Robert Shaw, described the sinking of the *USS Indianapolis* in the South Pacific near the end of World War II and the horrific scene of hundreds of American sailors consumed by sharks. He says that he was most afraid *after* rescuers came, that he would get this close to rescue and then be killed.

That feeling is precise. Then I was at the boat, and with a great groan, I leaped out of the water, fueled by terror and adrenalin, grasped the starboard rail, and vaulted almost completely over the deck and off the other side. I gasped and spat and sat, trembling uncontrollably while my friends started the boat and steered back toward the shark, screaming and banging on whatever was handy.

The shark, no doubt irritated, vanished, and my friends managed to haul on board what was left of the tarpon, still nearly 4 feet of fish. One friend's father would have it stuffed and mounted, and that half-fish would hang over his mantel for years to come.

I shook like a storm-lifted leaf for three straight hours.

And so this fog-smeared morning, I am thinking of the second verse in Genesis: "And the earth was without form and void; and darkness was upon the face of the deep. And the spirit of God moved upon the face of the waters."

Then the light: A thousand shafts of sun striking Florida Bay, ripping through the fog, which now melts. A wind rises from the calm and ruffles my hair, and I think of home and kin and a girl and days to come.

Idaho Springs, Colorado, 1997

It's a cold summer morning, and a mountain goat and I have been watching each other since first light. His head is spiked with shiv-like horns. I stand next to the rushing waters of Clear Creek, which runs clean and cold over time-smoothed stones. Just across the creek, a peak juts up abruptly, ready to catch the first sun.

Linda and I have come to Colorado to celebrate our twenty-fifth wedding anniversary, and she still sleeps. In a week, we will visit Aspen, Vail, Estes Park, and many other places. This is our second trip to Colorado in three years, and we have spent the night in a small, pleasant motel where she and our son came the summer before to mark his high school graduation.

Now, I squat and look at this curious goat, who is on a ledge a hundred feet above me just across the creek, impossibly nimble, stepping slowly over calving shale as if he were walking on a sidewalk. There are several females above and below him, along with a few bleating kids, impatient to hop from ledge to ledge. The mountain looms perhaps three or four hundred feet above the goats, spearing the mist like a cracker in milk.

I wear a heavy jacket, the collar turned up, and sip my coffee from a crockery mug and watch the cliffs for color.

First sun on the sea is a horizon event, but here light comes a long time before sun, and because we are in no hurry, I can await its slow transit. I know that my wife will still be wrapped in blankets and breathing lightly whenever I return. She is not fine-tuned to see each dawn as I am, and I envy her ability to sleep late and exult in the blankets of a cold morning.

The rocks on the shattered slopes in this light are slate gray but with a pale blue wash. Wisps of fog blow from peak to peak. The patriarch of this goatherd snorts out a challenge. Forget it, I say. I am the least nimble of men, prone to stumble. What he leaps across without waiting to see a landing sport would cast me downward to broken limbs or death.

An old man with whey-colored skin comes walking toward me grinning, his knotted legs strung down from rumpled khaki walking shorts. He bears coffee in a metal travel mug. The morning softens the desert terrain of his face, the arroyos and tectonic folds.

"Goats," I say, pointing at the cliffs across the creek. He grins, showing a mouthful of bad teeth. His face is impossibly long, the eyebrows unkempt brushwork.

"You watch them walk across?" he asks. "You'd break your neck taking one step, and they jump like it was nothing."

"I know it."

He's wearing a pale yellow jacket, and the steam from his coffee curls its tendrils up over his face. He's been bald a very long time. There is a look of utter satiety on his face, as if he were dying and yet in no pain and reflecting on a fantastically productive life.

"The sun will be over the peaks in a few minutes and then it creeps down all red and orange," he says. "It's a thing to see."

"I'm from Georgia," I say. He grins.

"I knew it was the South," he says. "That part was easy."

"Well."

"I'm from Wisconsin. Nothing like this in Wisconsin. Georgia, either, I bet."

"We have mountains, but they're much older than these. All the sharp edges worn down."

"Like me," he says. His eyes are wild with unspilled laughter. I cannot recall the last time I saw someone so pleased. "There." He points with a brief nod, and my eye crosses the stream and rises up past the sentinel goat, past the highest clear fault line and there, painted by numbers, is a slash of gold-orange just below the sharp blue sky.

Now, a cloud or mist bank passes, and a whisper of pale rose washes through the gold-orange. The old man slurps his coffee and watches it with pleasure. The stream sings with a constant *shushhhhhh*. We stand watching for nearly twenty minutes, silent, as the patriarch goat walks casually straight up the mountain, out for a morning stroll. He rises high enough to reach the light, and he is transformed into a dazzling pale ivory, with twin flames of steam spiking outward from his nostrils.

The old man comes toward me, and when he is alongside, he places his large arthritic hand on my shoulder and pats me once before heading back inside. I wonder if he has a wife or lover in there. A daughter, perhaps, come with him on a final journey to a beloved light.

Black Rock Mountain, Georgia, 1972

It rises more than 2000 feet over Clayton, a small town in far northeast Georgia, where I am editor of the *Clayton Tribune*. Atop Black Rock's rocky ledge there is a ranger station, since this is the highest state park in Georgia, and I have come to see the town below me, to inhale the fragrance of white pine and juniper.

This is my first job out of college, and I am frightened each day as I head for my small desk. I must write all the news, sell all the advertising, and put the paper together largely by myself. I am paid $110 a week for this. It is midsummer, and this morning, I have just arrived back from my usual weekend in Atlanta where I stay with Linda at her parents' home.

Months before, I had asked her to marry me when we were still students at the University of Georgia, and she said she couldn't answer that question. I said okay, I could wait. This weekend, out of the blue, she said, "I've been thinking about getting married."

"What have you decided?" I asked.

"That I want to," she said. And that was it, as much as a girl raised in New England wanted to discuss about the whole thing, except we both agreed the sooner the better. We are both twenty-two years old.

Now, on the cusp of a changed world, I have driven past the tiny, tin-roofed cabin where I live on the northern slope of Black Rock Mountain and come on up toward the sun. Each Monday morning, I rush back to Clayton for the workweek, but this morning I haven't gone to the office but instead straight up the mountain, where I park just as the sun rises.

The cabin is a pleasure, only four rooms (including the bathroom), facing east so that I can catch first light over a range of the southern Appalachians. Rain drums on the roof, and the windows shake in their frames when thunder comes. I feed apples, bought by the grocery bag from a roadside stand, to the horse that lives in a small pasture that rises up the hill behind me.

The road to the top of Black Rock is steep and winding but safe. I have parked near the ranger station and walked to the cliff-side expanse of clear stone.

"I am to be married," I say dramatically. It is our secret thus far, for we will wait a week or two before we speak of it to our families. Below me, morning is pouring into the valley, as if light had been dammed up and finally burst its barriers. I am already dressed uncomfortably for work, with my palm-wide necktie with the apple-sized knot. It is 1972, after all.

The air is chill and utterly unmoving. I try not to consider the unoriginal metaphorical baggage I hang on this morning and the beginning of my new life. Then I succumb to cliché. "I am to be married, and I will be a writer," I said. "I will write great poems and love my wife, and I will have children that I love."

Few things are more beautiful than ambition before first failure. I had already published a few poems in small magazines, but I had no idea how long the journey would be—another twelve years before my first book is published, a far longer gestation time than Emerson attributed to Whitman on first reading *Leaves of Grass*.

I had been surprised to find how poor a newspaper editor I was. I would get much better, but that, too, would take time. I worked miserably hard for another four years before I felt as if I had begun to master journalism.

Now, however, with the sun vibrating through deep green hemlock needles and their tiny brown cones, I feel a deep elation that I am capable of being loved by this woman I adore. Come late September, we will be married, and Linda will move with me to the cabin, where we will take turns sitting in the single chair we can afford.

Those children, too, will come, Brandon in 1978 and Megan in 1991. All my life, I will go back to that morning on Black Rock Mountain and with it mark far better days to come.

Manhattan, 1991

I awaken in the Penta Hotel, frightfully hung over, unable to sleep.

I throw my legs over the bed, wishing I could sleep at least until dawn, but it's hopeless: The genes will win every time. The night before, flush with a new contract from Random House, I went to a party to celebrate its glitzy new imprint, Turtle Bay Books.

I am virtually out of control. Yesterday, I had attended a session at the Jacob Javits Center in Manhattan of the American Bookseller Association's annual meeting, where I saw, standing back to back like different species, sex therapist Dr. Ruth Westheimer and basketball star Wilt Chamberlain. Neither knew the other was there, and they moved away from each other with their entourages.

I was celebrating the publication of my novel *Perfect Timing*, but I was also meeting Joni Evans, the editor of my new novel, *Final Heat*, which Turtle Bay Books would publish the next year. In midday, Joni and I took a cab to Turtle Bay's brownstone, where we worked on my manuscript for a while.

That night, I rode a taxi to the apartment of my then-literary agent Richard Murdoch in Midtown, where I managed to consume several bourbon and waters before heading for the party. At the party, I drank even more and wound up with my arm around the shoulder of an elderly gentleman.

"Jesus Christ, kid," said Richard, pulling me away. He called me *kid* even though I was older than he was, but Richard called everybody *kid*. "Don't you know who that was?"

"Who *who* was?"

"That guy you were slobbering all over," he said. "That was Si Newhouse. He owns all this." Richard made a grand gesture.

"The brownstone?" The name was starting to seem more familiar.

"No, moron, Random House and half of New York."

"Uh," I said.

Richard poured me into a cab, and we wound up at a Hard Rock Café around midnight, where I watched the waitresses go through a pretty good dance routine—only in New York. After a while, he carried me to a cab, told the driver where I was staying and looked at me with great relief through the window.

"Get there in one piece, kid," he said.

"Uh," I managed.

I lay in the back seat with my head looking upside down through the rear windshield, trying to pluck a few stars from the night sky.

Genetics, as I have said, will not let me sleep late, even when I've made an utter fool of myself. I awaken in the small room of the Penta just before dawn, fully aware of why most people hate morning. My head feels like the skin of a conga drum after a three-day song. I stagger to the bathroom, eat three Excedrins, then shower and go looking for a coffee shop.

A summer morning in Manhattan: the quiet roar of delivery trucks, the distant clankings of gears, the sound of a homeless man snoring as he leans against the cornice of the hotel. There's not a soul around Madison Square Garden across the street. I feel the usual remorse—I've always been a bad drinker—but even more, there's a volatile mixture of shame and sorrow. I walk down the street, pulling myself together, since later in the day I have to do an autographing at the ABA, but there's not much of me to pull. It's just light, and there's no mention yet of sun. This was in the days before Manhattan was emptied of trash and the homeless, but this morning, not even the drunks, druggies, deadbeats, and mentally ill roll over to beg for a quarter. I step over one man who is, I am quite certain, dead. I had been a newspaper reporter for years, though, and I've seen dead people—just enough to decide, again to my shame, that it's someone else's problem.

I come around a corner, and there, thank you God, is a coffeehouse, squatting on a corner like an Edward Hopper painting. A cab comes past me, its driver yawning and fooling with the radio knob. A young and apparently well-to-do couple, still in evening dress, is arguing like hell at the next corner. Scott and Zelda.

All I can think is that this is not my country. Still, I had seen my first novel in the window of the Scribner's Bookstore on Fifth Avenue, had tiptoed in the giant steps of Hemingway and Dreiser. I dreamed of my eternally beloved Whitman. So I try to remember how far I have come to be on this street, but my head throbs with the bass notes of the city.

Then, without a fanfare, a streak of sunlight paints itself across the spires of the skyscrapers, and I am breathless with love and admiration. The bandana of sunlight is orange and alizarin crimson, and I lean back against the quoins of some anonymous building and watch it move with Broadway élan down the slopes of brick and stone.

"You okay?" I turn to my left, and there's a jogger standing near me, glowing with sweat and health.

"Fine," I say. "I was just watching the sun rise. I'm not from around here. Where I'm from, there are mostly trees and things."

"You want trees, go to the park," he says, and he points north. He's not serious. "You look a little pale if you don't mind me saying so. I just thought—"

"I'm pale because I'm stupid," I say. "I'm going to get some coffee."

"Coffee gets rid of stupid," he says. "I'm a morning person myself." He jogs off, self-confident, self-important. I understand, perhaps for the first time, why so many people can't stand morning lovers.

In the coffee shop, I sit in the window and watch as the sunlight pours like a molten flood into Manhattan and the streets fill. Maybe I *will* take a cab to Central Park later in the day. I need something green.

Athens, Georgia, 1988

It's just after seven in the morning, and the phone is ringing. It's a fine Saturday in March, with a high blue sky I've already inspected from our deck. We live at the end of a dead-end street in the woods, and a small branch trickles steadily at the bottom of a sharp hill below us. It invites ribbons of sunlight and copperheads, two of which I've killed with a baseball bat over the past few years not 10 feet from our house.

This morning, I've already been up for two hours, working as always on a novel, listening to Mahler and Beethoven on my headphones. My study is in a loft with a huge window that opens over our den. The house is tiny, a dollhouse of a residence, the first home we've ever owned after years of renting and living near the poverty line. It's a modified A-frame, with shoulders like a barn's. Linda is sleeping in our king-sized waterbed, which takes up virtually the entire bedroom.

Brandon, our nine-year-old son, has spent the night in Madison, 30 miles south, with my mother and father. Though I had been editor of an alternative weekly newspaper for seven years, I am now a science writer at the University of Georgia, an eight-to-five job that I love. Things are looking up for us, since I have a new novel called *All the Western Stars* just about to come out, and two more slated for publication in quick succession after that. Linda is in the middle of a rewarding career teaching English to eighth graders.

I have done my usual thousand words on the new novel, fed our cats, and even slipped seed to our caged Society finch, Tristan, who lives in my study. I go on to the front driveway and shoot a few hoops. When I come back into the house, the phone is ringing. It's my mother.

"Phil?" she's saying. I don't have time to think anything. "Emma just called." She pauses only a moment. "Mama's gone."

I look at the sunlight that has worked its way through the window and smeared a golden streak across the top of our small piano.

"Oh no," I say. "No, no."

So, in the night, my grandmother, Lillie Mae Kirby Sisk, has died at the personal care home, run by a nice woman named Emma Kane, outside Athens. I had visited her every Monday for the past two years, and I can't quite think. I sit on the steps, breathless, thinking of my son, and the fact that he was with my mother when she found out *her* mother had died.

Linda hears the shock and alarm in my voice and comes hazily from the bedroom, questions in her eyes. I look up helplessly at her. My mother and father need to get to Emma's house, and they will meet us just outside Athens so we can pick up Brandon and they can go on to the personal care home. I hang up, shuddering.

"My grandmother died," I say, and I begin to cry, but only a little. I try to tell myself it isn't a tragedy when someone eighty-nine dies in her sleep. (Later we will find out that she was actually ninety-one.) Linda hugs me and holds me, and I shake it off. There will be a funeral. I am sure to be a pallbearer, which at first bothers me, but a few moments later I like the idea.

I tell her that I have to pick up Brandon at the Davis Brothers cafeteria just outside Athens so my mother and father can drive east to Emma's house.

"I'm so sorry," she says. Her comfort saves me, as it has my entire adult life.

Brandon, to my relief, is calm and fine, though sorrowful at the loss of his great-grandmother. My mother is holding her own as I get Brandon and bring him home. Once back, I get my shovel and begin to dig a large hole.

The slant of light rises slowly higher. I think of my grandmother, born in 1898, living through the Depression in the small mill town of Newry, South Carolina. I remember her calm quietness, her love of reading and crossword puzzles, her enduring dislike of old people. I dig. The hole is just next to the end of our driveway.

When I have it just so, I place a small Leyland cypress in the red dirt, pack it in, and then water it. I do the same thing on the other side of the driveway. I think: I had planned to plant these trees today for the landscape design I've been working on around the house. Now, they are memorials to someone I loved. *Grow*, I think. *Take the sunlight today and tomorrow and make something of yourselves.*

Fifteen years later, we live on Wildcat Ridge, in a house that befits our tenacity for saving money and my two jobs as a science writer and a novelist. We are still in the woods, and our 7 acres of land have their own evergreens, pine and red cedar. One morning, before work, I decide to drive by our old house, and when I arrive on Merlin Court west of Athens, the trees are stunning.

These twin green memories sway in the morning breeze, 30 feet tall, shaking off the light like rainwater. I turn into the driveway, back out like someone who has lost my way, and see the trees in my rear-view mirror as I drive away and into another day.

The Morning of Family

It is the middle of February 2004, and I am standing in the woods behind our house in my heavy blue coat, rearranging the shape of my family. We will be leaving soon for Athens Regional Hospital where my daughter-in-law, Laura Boyd, has been laboring mightily to deliver our first grandchild for more than a day. Brandon is to be a father for the first time.

The air seems to shimmer, clear and strong, as the first wisps of a rose tint come up from the east, back toward Mark's house and the Oconee River. There's something about that color...then I remember: stamp collecting. As boys, Mark and I bought packets of stamps from the H. E. Harris Company by mail, and stamp values were often determined by color—a rose "issue" might be worth far more than one to which a slight magenta was added after the first few thousand were printed. I attach exploratory ideas to color, dream of it in the same way I dreamed of stamps from the British Commonwealth as a boy.

I see the flapping outlines of crows as they bounce from limbs, swim through the under-canopy. The red-tailed hawks are already hunting, shrieking their *keeeer* as they rise and dive. It is the seventeenth of February, and today my life will change, just as each day the natural world is changed by morning. Today, Caleb Alden Williams will come into this world.

We almost never see birth in the natural world, and yet wrens fill their nests with eggs, raccoons hide themselves for birth, and egg sacs ripen and split, emitting tadpoles into the bronze-colored backwaters of creeks. Once, humans gave birth in shelters and then bedrooms, hidden, screams of the mother overlapping with crying babies or weeping relatives. Ernest Hemingway wrote a powerful story called "Indian Camp," in which his alter ego Nick Adams goes with his doctor father to attend an Indian woman who is in labor. After the child has been delivered and Nick's father has sewn her up with fishing line, they discover her husband, dead in the top bunk of their cabin, having been unable to bear her screams, dead from cutting his own throat. The story haunts us, and when the sun comes up, Nick isn't much happier at the horror he's seen:

They were seated in the boat. Nick in the stern, his father rowing. The sun was coming up over the hills. A bass jumped, making a circle in the water. Nick trailed his hand in the water. It felt warm in the sharp chill of the morning.

In the early morning on the lake sitting in the stern of the boat with his father rowing, he felt quite sure that he would never die.

Life these days is far easier, and we humans attend births as holy things, and babies come when they will, morning or night. This morning, however, they will induce Caleb's birth, or at least that's the plan, because Laura, in labor for more than twenty-four hours, has been unable to deliver the child. So we know that Caleb will see *his* first light not long after the *day's* first light, and I love the symmetry.

Babies cannot see far for several weeks, but if Caleb saw these woods on the morning of his birth, he would see this: gray, gray, and gray—trunks of white oak, tulip poplar, American beech, dogwood, hickory, pine, and sweet gum. He would see the watercolor image of new light on the long strips of dead bark that peel off like ribbons from the red cedar that long ago died but refuses to fall or even drop its limbs. He would see the earth's brown floor of leaf litter or silver-white beech leaves that refuse to fall. He would see green, too: mosses and lichens that enjoy the damp coolness on huge exposed rocks that nose up from the soil down toward our creek; the shoots of wild onions, oblivious to the cold; nubs of jonquils, early blades of irises knifing through the hard earth.

Just before dawn, the birds begin their songs—how long could it be, really, until spring? Are they testing morning songs to see what sounds they get in return? No, spring is still some time yet, and for now, the morning is cold enough for me to leave the light on in our well house. (One light bulb can keep such a small space quite warm even on a very cold night, one well below freezing.) A cow across Oliver Bridge Road is lowing, speaking in those sweet hollow syllables that sound like longing.

This part of the Earth's curved continents is turning ponderously toward the sun. All day, all night, we are spinning, but we never know it. The Christian church, until well into the Renaissance, denied what did not conform to its ideas of this world. Surely the Earth was the center of the universe. Surely the sun and the heavens turned around Earth. Well, no. Surely storms and earthquakes were God's punishment for wickedness. Surely, surely, surely.

Old ideas, especially those borne of religious certainty, die hard. Evil things occurred at night, and the morning revealed truths, even epiphanies. Even now, walking alone at night brings fear to most people—fear of muggings in the city or suburbs, or of snakes and coyotes where I live. And yet we have turned into a nation of nighthawks as the farmer's idea of working from light to light has almost vanished from America.

Mariners still say, "Red in the morning, sailors take warning; red at night, sailors delight." It's the equivalent of reading tealeaves or carrying a rabbit's foot.

I have taught creative writing to college students, and from time to time, I ask my students whether they are a morning person or night person? The response is usually a laugh and some response such as "Are you kidding?" Perhaps our constructs of morning depend on our age after all—as children we are to bed early. As teenagers and young adults, we almost never see early morning. Then when we pass fifty, morning seems, perhaps, a kind thing again. Maybe it is because we sleep poorly or because we are greedy to see another day. More likely, it's a simple shift in metabolism that allows us to get by on less sleep, to rise even when we'd like to sleep in.

Sometimes the world changes in the morning: September 11, 2001. But more often, we pass most mornings of our lives the way we pass most evenings: too busy to notice what either means.

A red-bellied woodpecker hammers on a tree, pausing to hoot merrily. Sing, I want to say, for the coming of my new generations.

My daughter Megan and I arrive at the hospital where my wife has spent the night in a chair, waiting for Caleb to be born. Laura's mother, Lorene, and her friend Melissa are also there, exhausted from waiting and worrying. It's just after seven, and the day's new light streaks through the hospital's entrance atrium.

"What's happening?" I ask. Others are here, waiting, exulting. Linda looks wary, strong.

"They've decided to do a C-section," she says. "He's just not going to be born any other way. They're prepping her now."

I chat with Lorene, and she is excited and nervous. I feel strange, twisted up inside, seeing years stretch before me with a tow-headed grandson, of fishing trips, of introductions to Mahler and Monet and morning, to trips up Black Rock Mountain to see the sun swell in magnificence over North Georgia.

There's an odd lapse in my family's relationship to country and its natural wonders. My father was a town kid, born and raised in Seneca, South Carolina, and my mother came from the tiny nearby mill village of Newry, though at fifteen she moved to Seneca with her family. So neither of them was really a country kid, though my father had numerous relatives in the rural areas of Oconee County, South Carolina. Mark and I, however, came of age in what was then the country on the outskirts of Madison, Georgia, where our father was principal of Morgan County High School and our mother was later co-owner of a kindergarten named Magic Land. Our younger sister, Laura Jane, was born while we lived in the country but was still a toddler when we moved into Madison in 1961.

Since then, Mark and I have been obsessed with country, with the remains of the natural world, and my fascination with morning began in that precious country of youth. So Caleb's great-grandparents on my side were city-dwellers while his grandfather was a country child who grew into a countryman. (My wife Linda is a child of the suburbs, from Boston, Atlanta, and New Jersey.) Lineage is a strange trail with many twists.

I sit down in the waiting room. All the babies born the day before and in the night have been taken to their mothers, so the nursery, with its broad plate-glass observation area, is empty now. People coming to work bring tidings of the February morning with them—coats, mufflers, pinked cheeks, good mornings. I close my eyes and think:

Dear Caleb,

This morning rose with a thin sun, cold and foggy over Wildcat Ridge, and I went outside thinking about you as Megan dressed. I smelled wood-smoke adrift from someone's fire, saw gray on gray from the forest's tree trunks, heard the squirrels arguing over the huge pan of birdseed Linda puts out. Before dark yesterday, I looked out the kitchen window and saw the pan full of sparrows, as if ready to slide in an oven and bake.

Morning is my true north. I have never been a creature of the night, though I have loved it in its parts. One of my favorite writers, Loren Eiseley, said in his book *The Night Country*:

"This is your house," says the poet Conrad Aiken, and you know he is talking about the human skull. "On one side there is darkness," he warns you; "on one side there is light."

Your grandmother made me see Eiseley more clearly in about 1970 when we were college students, falling in love with each other and the world of ideas. If I have chosen the light over the darkness, it is a choice mediated by genes. I am a morning person not by choice but by selection.

Your first day was a cold one in North Georgia. The first light I saw when I let our beagle Murphy, out for the morning was the glow from inside the well house. But presently, the earth turned farther toward the sun, and the shapes of my world began to redefine themselves as they do each morning.

Much of the living world is asleep this time of year. The peepers don't peep. Our bulb plants have barely broken through the cold dirt. Crows flop and flap, coughing reticently. When cold fronts come through, the turkey vultures (a nicer name than the coarser "buzzards") throw themselves into the air and labor upward to reach the northwesterlies. In the summer, they ride for hours on thermals, angling in taut circles over carrion, making clean white bones of the dead.

This is not a morning of leaving, though, but of your arrival. I walked in the edge of the woods and placed my nose to the trunk of a white oak and inhaled: the rich scent of cold bark, like a distant memory, brought back but mysterious. Someday I'll tell you about Proust's *madelaine*. Then I see it: the upper trunks painted with pale lemon yellow, sunstrokes on the narrowing bodies of hickory and elm. The forest shifts into shadows. (On moony nights, the forest also has shadows, but these are different, denser, almost dimensional. Those shadows lack much color.) Morning brings shapes and sundry movements among the leaf litter.

Who else first saw light on this date? The Italian composer Archangelo Corelli in 1753. Writer Dorothy Canfield Fisher in 1879. Red Barber, the best baseball announcer of all time, in 1908. Hal Holbrook. Michael

Jordan. Rene Russo. Huey Newton. And events: the 100th anniversary of the premiere of *Madama Butterfly*. The burning of Columbia, South Carolina, during the Civil War. That town is still too hot even to visit in the summer. Maybe someday the very old Michael Jordan will take note of the fact he was born on the same day as Caleb Williams.

Winter is a country of twigs. Deadfall litters the forest floor from cold fronts and natural deaths. Just before the steep slope falls off into Wildcat Creek, there is a complete deer skeleton, and this morning, its bones were bathed in that same lemon yellow of sunrise, quite beautiful really.

Your two grandmothers are in this room. They are teachers. Your mother's mother teaches hearing-impaired children and loves to ride bikes with her friends. Your father's mother has taught eighth-grade English for some twenty-eight years.

I'm a writer and composer, and in ancient history would, perhaps, have been a scribe. Strange, but I was born in the early afternoon, my least-favorite time of day. Perhaps we grow allergic to the time we leave the safety of the womb. That seems laughable, illogical, mythic, but stranger things have been proved true.

This world is an unholy mess. Some men start wars, slaughter each other, kill the animals, and cut old-growth forests. Some drill fragile wildlife areas for oil we could spare if we'd only conserve a little. Our current government has cut-and-spent us into a debt that is beyond comprehension. But do not get the idea that I am guiltless. We are all humans, and despite wonderful accomplishments (check out Van Gogh and

Michelangelo when you get a little older), we are wreckage on the world's morning shore.

But you will emerge from your cocoon this morning to multiple threads of love. You are a lucky boy. I am waiting.

Love,

Papa

The phone rings. It's our son Brandon saying that they've taken Laura into surgery already, and we bustle around, edging our worry with excitement. When babies come into the viewing area, they're brought by nurses—with one exception. Since the doctors are stitching and cleaning C-section mothers, the fathers can come, in scrubs, into the nursery with their newborn babes, showing them off to admiring family. We huddle by the large plate-glass window.

I am thinking of something that happened to me almost exactly ten years ago to the day in this same hospital. My heart's mitral valve was falling apart, and I was headed for congestive heart failure and an early death. One generation earlier, and I've have been dead within eighteen months. (The great composer Gustav Mahler, one of my artistic gods, died of an infected mitral valve in 1911 at the age of fifty.) Now, I have a mechanical valve and an 8-inch scar down the middle of my chest, but I'm very much alive and fifty-four years old. It occurs to me that modern medicine—the now-common C-section—is saving the lives of Laura and Caleb, too. A century before, neither might have made it through the ordeal.

Suddenly, like a primary school play, curtains are drawn shut across the window of the nursery, and we walk away, sit down nervously, and look at each other. Five minutes pass, seven. Then there's a swoosh, the curtains part rapidly, and there is Brandon in scrubs, smiling broadly, standing over an utterly naked and crying Caleb in his medical bassinet, which lies beneath a warmer.

I put my hand on Linda's shoulder: It is another morning of our lives, 8:52 A.M., and Caleb Alden Williams is here to grow into our stories. I love the morning, baseball, classical music, art history, baseball and football, poetry, and fiction. Linda loves the night, football, Westerns, Alaska, and Golden Oldies rock. He'll hear Beethoven from me and "Happy Together" by the Turtles from my wife.

Sentimentalism is the great killer of writing. And most people would probably agree with Joy Behar that they would shoot 5:00 A.M. if they saw it on the street. But for me, it's a lovely cold memorable precious delightful morning.

A Morning for the Stones

Spring has returned to the South. My father and I have come this bright, nearly cloudless morning to love our family stones. We've driven from Georgia to Northwestern South Carolina and stand in the churchyard of South Union Baptist Church. It's just after nine, and no one else is anywhere in sight. Birdsong fills the space between the gravestones: cardinal, chickadee, nuthatch, mockingbird. We've come to see if the marker for Elijah Land still stands.

The sunlight casts sharp shadows from the headstones, wide and low, tall and spiked—the dead lie in military lines. How much better if we simply scattered our dead in random patterns around a hillside! We see death as unnatural, though, and we must try to arrange our ancestors as if death could be reshaped.

Elijah Land is the grandfather of Isabel Williams—my father's mother. Old Elijah, therefore is one of my great-great-grandfathers. His first wife was one Eleanor Jolly, but when she died, he married again.

"Boy, what a morning," I say as we walk slowly across the cemetery. "Couldn't have picked a better day."

"Isn't it nice?" my father says.

It's cool, perhaps 50 degrees, and a slight wind gives the chill a pleasant, breathing edge. I never knew my father's mother or father—they both died before I was born. The grass is brown, and crows make their presence known. My father hadn't even made the connection between our family and Elijah Land until a few years back, and when he found the man's stone at South Union, it was broken into three pieces. At first, he simply cemented the pieces together and stood it back up, but that wasn't enough, so he wired twin rods, copper-sheathed iron, to either side of the monument to keep it upright. My father, the college chemistry major, knows that iron rods will eventually stain marble; copper won't. Smart man. We've come to see if the stone is still standing.

Elijah was born on May 8, 1796, and died on May 10, 1884. I try to do the chronologies in my head: he was alive with George Washington and Beethoven. He was an old man when the Civil War came, then kept living for nearly twenty years after the country was sutured back from its collective madness. His blood flows in my veins. He was a farmer like most of my kin, and morning to him would have meant a cup of strong coffee and heading off to the sweet smell of horseflesh, the aroma of upturned soil this time of year. His second wife, Elizabeth, is buried beside him. My father has no memory of his own mother ever mentioning the man, who died before she was born. Daddy discovered our relation when searching through census records.

"I just found this out not too long ago, but Elijah's father was Joseph Land, Jr.," says my father. "His father was Senior, of course, and Senior died in 1803."

The stone is marble, and lichen has crawled in pleasant patterns along the surface, in love with the rock's lime content. Water stains trail across the grains. A dried oak leaf landed between one rod and the tombstone, and I remove it, let it flutter to the ground.

We walk around the South Union churchyard for a while, visiting the graves of Jolly ancestors. One, John Jolly, was born in 1784—when Jefferson and Adams were forming a new nation.

My car cuts through a South Carolina morning. Leaves have not yet begun to open on the trees, so it feels like spring, but looks like winter. We arrive at the graveyard of the First Baptist Church of Westminster, South Carolina. We have come to the graves of David W. Jaynes and Maggie Bearden Jaynes, my great-grandparents. Faded cloth roses lie across David's grave. He died on April 22, 1931—the same day and month that my father's father would die four years later. Cars are stirring by now, knitting the centerline of a nearby highway. My father casually identifies stones right and left belonging to those related to us, either directly or by marriage. We pass some Tannery dead.

"Three Land sisters married three Tannery brothers, so we're kin to them," my father explains. He doesn't have to point out the parallel to me: my grandmother and two of her Jaynes sisters married the three Williams brothers, creating a tangle of double first cousins. We come across Thomas F. McGuffin, who's also kin—our ties to the McGuffins go back to Ireland in the eighteenth century. The cemetery is full of cedar trees, and I express admiration.

My father is dubious.

"Cemeteries," he says, "do not need any kind of trees."

"I don't agree. I think they're nice."

"No. They tear up the place."

We come upon the grave of Thomas A. Williams, the brother of my father's grandfather. A cedar tree is starting to turn the marker over, making my argument look more specious by the minute. Water-oak leaves crackle under foot. Sunlight twinkles on the stones. We browse names. Clifton H. King and his wife, Annie, are buried nearby. The lived next door to my father when he was a boy in Seneca, South Carolina, in the '20s and '30s.

"He was the most gentle man I've ever known," says my father, deep in thought. "He was the one who worked at the railroad depot and let me use the telegraph key. He was a railroad telegrapher. When I was a boy, he worked at night and sometimes paid me to go spend the night in his house because his wife was afraid of being alone. Fifty cents a night. I remember sitting out on the porch talking to her not long after he died. They never had any children."

And so we have come to the center of my father's dead: the Return Baptist Church Cemetery. This is where he and my mother will be buried, in the same plot with his parents and my Uncle Cecil—yet another relative who died before I was born. They're logging across the road, scarring up the land. The stench of diesel smoke fills the air. Fully one-fifth of those buried in this cemetery are related to me—more than thirty people. When I was a boy, this church was deep in the country, but now the world is closing in. The roaring of machinery annoys me.

My father walks around the plot spraying stray clumps of dandelions and other weeds with weed killer. My grandfather's grave is slightly sunken, cupping shadow as the sun gets higher in the morning.

"You're going to be buried right next to Cecil, and mother will be on the other side of you," I say.

"Right," he said, not a trace of sentiment in his voice. "See to it."

"I will."

At the foot of my grandparents' plot are my great-uncle Barrington Avery Williams and his wife Flora. Saddled his long life with such a fancy name, my great-uncle went by the nickname "Tack." My father doesn't seem to remember how he got the name. I remember the last time I saw him—in bed with cancer toward the very end of his life forty years ago. He couldn't move. Now, I think, with the words honed by centuries of others, he's "at rest."

The sky fills with fair-weather cumulus clouds. My Uncle Cecil died sixty years ago—my father's sensitive, artistic older brother. I watch my father spray weeds.

"I'll make this my avocation," I say after a moment. "I'll be the one to do this, to keep this place clean and neat."

"All right," my father says.

⁕

We walk around the cemetery after finishing with the plot and putting down fresh cloth flowers at the headstones of my grandmother and grandfather. Even after my mother and father are buried here, there will be one space left empty. My father says we can all come if we get cremated—room for ten more.

Some of my relatives have only fieldstones, and the inscriptions are fading rapidly. In the sharp light of this morning, I can read one, barely make out name and date. We come from the poor, but at least music ran through their veins far, far back, and I have that heritage, and now my son and daughter do. Linda and I have promised Brandon and Laura that we will buy Caleb's first cello—the instrument they want him to play and that Brandon himself played. (My grandfather Williams, buried here, played fiddle in a mountain string band, and Laura teaches private violin lessons from her house.)

A distant cousin—Lee Williams—has a fancy marker, but his body wasn't even here for two years after he died. He was in the Second Company, Coast Guard Artillery C, and died when the transports *Otranto* and *Kashmir* collided off the coast of Scotland near the end of World War I. His body wasn't returned until late summer 1920, where it was reinterred.

All across this place, my ancestors' stones gleam in the morning light. All the marble and granite markers are straight up and in rows, but the fieldstones lie at many angles, casting strange angular shadows.

This morning with my father ebbs toward noon. We drive through the countryside toward Seneca and Mountain View Cemetery, where more relatives lie. The road curls around back, and we park within 2 feet of my mother's parents, Lee and Lily Sisk. He died in 1969, she in 1988. Down the slope are an aunt and uncle, Vincent A. Williams, called Sambo, and his wife, known always as Mac.

So many stones, so many shadows. I try to let this morning sink into me, enjoy the birds, watch the high cirrus, crystal feathers far beyond the puffs of cumulus. All things have their mornings, even the dead. And if these names all converge into a town of the lost, that town is ours, too, and we walk among them, and memory becomes part of who we remain.

We don't feel sad, aren't especially solemn or reflective. Since I was a boy, I have tramped cemeteries with my father, looking for relatives or the famous, reading epitaphs, speculating on lives. This morning, we feel close. I feel as if we could talk for days without running out of things to say.

I am fifty-four, and he is eighty-one.

He walks through one section, remembering people from seventy years past, quirks of their lives, fine qualities, the things one recalls. He points out the stone of a Mrs. Grissop. After her husband died decades ago, she made hats for women to keep food on the table. My father as a boy had a job in this cemetery—in the 1930s—cleaning tombstones. The only problem was that he used hydrochloric acid, which eats marble. (He would later major in chemistry at the University of Georgia after World War II.)

Mr. Frank Holleman is buried here just above the access road. He was a banker. One day, my father's father, Arthur S. Williams, went into the bank and withdrew his life savings—an amazing $2000. He said he didn't really trust banks anymore. This was, of course, during the Depression. (My grandfather died in 1935 at the age of forty-three.)

"Arthur, I have always thought you were a good citizen, and I really hate to see you taking all your money out," Mr. Holleman said. My grandfather nodded but said little. He was a quiet man. My father takes up the story.

"Daddy went ahead and took the money out, but he brought it back the next day," he says.

"I want to make a deposit," my grandfather said. "Mr. Holleman, you've been a good citizen, too, and we will sink or swim together."

My father never heard the story until perhaps thirty years after the event, when the very aged Holleman stopped him on the streets in Seneca one day and repeated it, still strong in his memory.

Morning is gone. It's early afternoon, and we sit next to my father's aunt, Lucille Spencer, who lies in her nursing home bed, body wracked but mind still completely clear at age ninety-one. She remembers my grandfather clearly—a man now dead nearly seventy years.

"Is it snowing?" she asks, looking out the window. My father and I turn and see the petals from a Bradford pear tree blowing past in the sharp sunlight. Lucille's eyes are lit from within. She repeats family stories, tells secrets, knows, utterly, where she is, who we are. She will pass away the following year.

Morning is not just a time of day. It is a map toward memory and family, and its gentle chains bind us to all of our past, even the part we never knew.

Mornings of the World

I typed the word "morning" into Google and got 667 million hits back. I didn't look through all of them. In fact, I looked at virtually none of them. Morning is ubiquitous, for Pete's sake—every day has a morning, even those before we are born and after we die. There are mornings on other planets. I was once a reporter and producer for an agricultural television show called *Georgia Morning*. It aired at 6:00 A.M. on Georgia Public Television, at a time when farmers might be finishing their coffee and preparing for fieldwork.

We don't think about morning as a ripe subject for thought because of its very commonness. It's like writing about Tuesday. And yet there's a landscape of morning, an etymology. Morning has its own art, its appeal to all the senses.

I have lived only in Georgia, and north central Georgia at that, except for six months in the mountains. I don't know South Georgia as nature writers Janisse Ray or Amy Blackmarr do. The geography of my life has been sharply circumscribed because I've never wanted to drift very far from my home territory. Whenever I'm away, I'm plotting timesaving measures to return more quickly than I'd planned.

Though I'm a world traveler compared to Emily Dickinson, and I could never be a tenth the artist she was, I don't think understanding a place and integrating it with life is something easily done. In fact, I doubt many people give a passing thought to things that puzzle many people for decades.

I began to think about morning as a boy, since it was the time of day I felt most alive. There was a fertility to my thinking in the morning, an edge to my dreams. When I got to college, I was an oddball in those days of hippies and the Vietnam War. I met Linda because she was late arriving at a biology lab, bleary-eyed at 8:00 A.M., while I sat there bright-eyed as a puppy. Everybody smoked and spent their first fifteen minutes of morning learning to breathe again. We were political and ardent—but no one had a fiery anti-war meeting at 8:00 A.M.

Morning has always started for me in darkness. In the past three decades, I have risen after dawn less than five times. Sometimes, in warm weather, I will go outside and try to navigate in that darkness, to see what separates it from the night. In the film *Witness*, Harrison Ford's character is eating breakfast in the pre-dawn hours with his Amish hosts—he's a Philadelphia cop who knows too much about his crooked colleagues. He's sitting wanly as his host, old Mr. Lapp, asks if he doesn't like breakfast. Ford replies, "Not in the middle of the night." For most people 4:15—the time I arise many days—*is* the middle of the night. But for me it's a different territory.

Spring is coming again, and I'm still here to witness it, still a son, a brother, a husband, a father, and now a grandfather. So I edge outside just as the sun is rising along the hillsides of this country.

This land has seen millions of years, and mornings by the tens of millions, and yet each day—like each snowflake—is different. During the night, new sticks of deadfall may have littered the forest floor. The dunes beneath the flowing waters of Wildcat Creek have shifted all night, sinuous as a desert sidewinder. Soon the leaves will come out on the hickories, the poplars, the white oaks, the large elm by our front porch. An anole on our rotting woodpile peers east, waiting for the sun.

Sounds are different. At 5:43 A.M., a crow barks gently. Our neighborly red-shouldered hawk lifts off a tree limb, plump as a turkey, and glides through the under-canopy, surely a menacing presence to rodents but lovely to me. The wind is utterly calm, as if the earth were holding its breath. The air is cool and heavy with humidity. A squirrel scratches along the trunk of a bold oak, walking straight up and out of sight.

Much remains unseen. The raccoons are still active at this hour at the creek, the deer already moving. When the light comes, I can walk to the creek and find tracks so fresh you can almost smell who made them, small pawed prints that end with claw tracks or heart-shaped doe patterns. Opossums are about—we haven't seen any around our house in several years now, but they're out there. All night, as the soil warms, hundreds of species of insects grow more active, and the rich forest soil boils with earthworms, those ubiquitous friends that so fascinated Darwin.

Now, there's a change. The earth moves around ponderously, and this small patch of land begins to face toward the sun. The air feels cooler, but it is not cold; spring is nearing these late days in March. I can see the outlines of trees first, slate black against the contours of the hill. An enormous dead cedar has stood in the same place for more than a decade, showing no signs of rotting or falling. It is more like a monument than a living thing whose organic electricity has been shut off. The tree is on the eastern edge of our land, right up to the property line. I see light through its proudly inert shape.

The dogwoods are beginning to leaf. There's one, and then another. Now I can see the sky, and it's streaked with stratocumulus clouds, and they grow rosy, like a girl's winter cheeks. I realize, too, that I am part of this emerging landscape.

J. A. Baker speaks eloquently about how we must walk through the landscape and not frighten the native fauna in his book *The Peregrine*: "A peregrine fears nothing he can see clearly and far off. Approach him across open ground with a steady unfaltering movement. Let your shape grow in size but do not alter its outline. Never hide yourself unless concealment is complete. Be alone. Shun the furtive oddity of man, cringe from the hostile eyes of farms. Learn to fear. To share fear is the greatest bond of all."

I have tried this for years, and for the most part it works. But animals flee also from noise, even though they become tamed by routine. An example: I arrive on the University of Georgia campus each morning at 7:00 A.M., and in the wintertime, it's dark. The rest of the year, the sun is up. For the past few days, the North Campus Quad has been alive with robins—dozens of them. They seem morbidly obese, but that's probably my chastened American eye telling me that.

Squirrels, accustomed to hundreds of students flowing past like a human river, don't mind my presence, hop past me on the sidewalks. In front of my building, there's a small hole at the edge of the sidewalk, and a chipmunk waits for me each morning, sitting up like a prairie dog in the grass, and then pouring himself down the hole at the penultimate moment. When the gingko tree begins to leaf, squirrels hang in it, gnawing away at the new life. One morning when I arrived, I counted nine squirrels in the tree.

"So that's where you guys come from," I said out loud. They didn't even lift their heads when I passed. Since then, I've always considered it the Squirrel Tree and pretend that, when mature, the squirrels drop off and scamper away.

So where do I fit in this landscape of morning? I can't say, after more than half a century of them, that I know. Barbara Kingsolver in her book *High Tide in Tucson* says that "It's starting to look as if the most shameful tradition of Western civilization in our need to deny we are animals." She's right, of course. We seem to believe that we are *separate* and *above* and therefore not part of the natural laws that regulate other animals on the planet. We are vastly different, for sure. With a large brain and opposable thumbs, we've managed to make wonderful things. Every time I look upon photographs of Michelangelo's *Pietá*, I find my eyes sodden with tears—not from religious ecstasy but from pride that I am a brother animal to the one who made *that*.

We, as a species, however, are prone to so many serial stupidities, so many episodes of pillaging of land and life, that I often wish I were a mollusk. Inventing an excuse for war is the easiest pastime on earth. Ignoring global warming, clear-cutting old-growth forests, draining wetlands—our kind are also hideously stupid simply because many of us believe we are gods of the land.

We aren't. We don't possess land any more than we own the sunrise. It possesses us, and we damn well better start listening to it.

So, there is an etymology of morning. This delicious time of day has its own religion and its own art. It brings joys and hangovers. Many of us have been selected to thrive in the early day, and others can't function in it. And yet I have a suspicion that we know more about the fruit fly genome than we know about the shape of morning. Morning is the day's new skin, shed each noon, and to many people it's no more than the time for alarm clocks and coffee. It doesn't have meaning, or if it does, that meaning is vague, full of stretching and yawning.

Each day when I rise, I wonder, How many more mornings will I be granted? Should I forget work and sit in the woods below me and watch the dawn slowly paint itself down the trunks and along my paths to Wildcat Creek? As always, Emerson got it right in *Nature*:

"To speak truly, few adult persons can see nature. Most persons do not see the sun. At least they have a very superficial seeing. The sun illuminates only the eye of man, but shines into the eye and the heart of a child. The lover of nature is he whose inward and outward senses are still truly adjusted to each other; who has retained the spirit of infancy even into the era of manhood."

Perhaps that sense of wonder is enough. I do know one thing. Children are not amazed to see another morning, as those my age sometimes are. We mark what we have lost on long solitary evenings, and we await the long roll call of our ancestors, urging us into the past as well.

While I live, while I can look out, if only from a window, morning is a gift for my survival. And in its geography, I find, every day, a glimmer of hope. And on many days, that hope leads me on its hidden trails toward joy.

Author's Note

Although all the people in this book are real, I have changed the names of several of them in order to protect their privacy.

I'd like to thank Dr. Roberto Refinetti of the University of South Carolina for his excellent assistance on the chapter about circadian rhythms; my brother, Dr. Mark Williams, for reading and commenting on the chapter about our canoe trip; and my father for letting me audio tape our trip to the South Carolina cemeteries.

The support of my literary agent, Bill Contardi, means a great deal to me, as it always does. He supported this book from the beginning. I'd also like to thank Marc Jolley of Mercer University Press for his belief in the manuscript.

Thanks as well to all the students at the University of Georgia who have studied nature writing with me over the past few years. You have been my inspiration.

Finally, I am blessed with a wonderful family. To my parents, my sister and brother, Laura Jane and Mark, thank you with all my heart. My debts to Linda, Megan, Brandon, Caleb, and Laura are likewise incalculable.